The Manager's Phrase Book

3,000+ Powerful Phrases That Put You in Command in Any Situation

By Patrick Alain

CAREER
PRESS
Pompton Plains, NJ

THE MANAGER'S PHRASE BOOK
EDITED BY KIRSTEN DALLEY
TYPESET BY DIANA GHAZZAWI
Cover design by Jeff Piasky
Printed in the U.S.A.

To order this title, please call toll-free 1-800-CAREER-1 (NJ and Canada: 201-848-0310) to order using VISA or MasterCard, or for further information on books from Career Press.

CAREER
PRESS

The Career Press, Inc.
220 West Parkway, Unit 12
Pompton Plains, NJ 07444
www.careerpress.com

Library of Congress Cataloging-in-Publication Data
Alain, Patrick.
    The manager's phrase book : 3,000+ powerful phrases that put you in command in any situation / by Patrick Alain.
        pages cm
    Includes index.
    ISBN 978-1-60163-246-3 -- ISBN 978-1-60163-552-5
        1. Business communication. 2. Management. 3. Conversation. I. Title.

HF5718.A3697 2013
658.4'5--dc23

                                                                    2012033811

Acknowledgments

First of all, I would like to express gratitude to Bassam and Lina Abi-Samra and profound appreciation to my magnificent wife, Zaina, for their unwavering support during the year it took me to write this book.

Next, I would be remiss if I did not thank my mother, Jacqueline, for all of her sacrifices. She has been my inspiration even before I ever knew I needed an inspiration. *Je t'aime, maman.*

I would also like to give special appreciation to Tom Carroll and Yesha Raval for their extraordinary contributions to the creativity represented in this work.

With deepest thanks I also recognize my agent, Jessica Faust; my developmental editor, Kirsten Dalley; and my publicist, Tess Woods.

Without these people, who were so generous with their time, commitment, and energy, this book would never have been possible.

Contents

Preface

Are you a purchasing manager, a production manager, or an IT manager? Do you manage in marketing, sales, or finance? Is it up to you to take charge of human resources or product development? Regardless of your industry or level of experience, you have to make optimum use of all the resources you have at your disposal. Being thrust into an unpredictable situation can be difficult, and this is doubly true when you are a manager. Regardless of whether you are a seasoned manager or someone who has not yet experienced all the power, perils, and pitfalls of leading people, you will be expected to take charge and make things better for your direct reports and the company. This balancing act isn't always easy, and it can be especially stressful if you are fumbling for words or lacking in nuance in your communications. The fact that you reached for this book means that you probably aren't satisfied with how you've been handling this aspect of your job. You know you can do better, but you need some magic phrases to help kick-start the process. And because you're busy, you need a reference tool that is concise, easy to use, and portable. In this book you'll find hundreds of specific responses that have helped managers and would-be managers just like you take control of their communications.

My goal in writing this book was to share these talking points so that you can develop a strong and capable managerial presence in *any* situation. The higher up you move in the chain of command, the more readily you will need to be able to summon powerful and effective words and phrases—to motivate, to inspire, to correct, to command. Ideally they should become second nature, a part of your everyday routine. To help you do that, this book is organized into 10 easy-to-digest sections, plus one bonus section at the end. There is also a comprehensive index at the end to help you locate relevant topics easily.

The fact is, no matter how successful or seasoned you are as a manager—or even if you've never managed before in your life—chances are your communication skills could use some polishing. This invaluable tool will enhance your command of the idiom and allow your confidence and managerial skills to shine through. You will find it incredibly rewarding, both personally and professionally, as you learn to speak boldly, persuasively, and, perhaps most of all, appropriately in any situation.

Let our journey to managerial confidence begin!

How to Use This Book

This book was designed with flexibility in mind. You can read it all the way through to get a general overview, or you can work on one particular situation or aspect of communication that you find the most challenging or relevant. For example, you may feel very comfortable talking to an employee about a personal problem, but you may not feel as relaxed when doling out criticism. Use the in-depth Index at the back to help you find the topic that is most applicable to your situation.

Read all the sample phrases and make a point to familiarize yourself with the ones that seem the most natural or comfortable for you. Then practice them until they flow naturally from your mouth. When the time comes you'll have no trouble summoning them and using them with confidence and aplomb. And because everyone says things in a slightly different way, there's a bit of space in the margins where you can add your own favorite catch phrases. The right words are not enough, however. Remember that tone, body language, and timing (context) are all important in conveying meaning and in how your statements are perceived by others. Thus, a humorous phrase that would be effective and appropriate in one setting could be construed as hostile and inappropriate in another, depending on how, when, and to whom it is said. Use good judgment and let context be your guide. This is particularly important when you are considering using humor or sarcasm to make a point. Humor can sometimes come across as flip or dismissive, and sarcasm is definitely one of the quickest ways to make someone feel inept. Not everyone will appreciate your style of delivery, so nuance is always required.

Conciliatory

Argumentative

The indicator accompanying each situation will help you anchor each "order of magnitude" in your mind, which will serve as a valuable mnemonic device down the road. For example, in the sample to the left, the continuum indicator goes from **Conciliatory** to **Argumentative**. All of the phrases in this book are presented on a similar scale. In this example, if you wanted to build bridges and/or smooth things over, you would learn and use the phrases toward the top. If you wanted to eliminate the niceties and cut to the chase—and maybe even wield your words as you would a weapon—you would use the phrases toward the bottom.

Finally, I thought it important to note that I am embracing the English language as most people understand and use it in America today; thus, the reader will find colloquialisms and some slang. Obviously, the vagaries of expression will be much different in, say, Canada or Australia, as they will be even in different parts of the States. Ultimately, the English language, like all languages, is a living thing; it is in constant flux. Therefore I'm prepared for the fact that the material in this book will need updating from time to time, as the way we express ourselves inevitably evolves.

Please visit my Website, *www.patrickalain.com*, for the most up-to-date information to add to your linguistic arsenal. I also welcome your comments on and criticisms of this work to help me in that process.

Part 1
Staffing and HR

A leader is a dealer in hope.
—Napoleon Bonaparte

Bringing in and acclimatizing new hires can be either your easiest or your most difficult task as a manager, depending on your industry, the available talent pool, your department's budget, your own skills and experience, and the overall culture of your company. But there's just no getting around it: This is an essential part of any manager's job. Each time you meet with a candidate or a new hire, you are working with a clean slate. Even if that person has pored over your LinkedIn profile page, he or she likely has little to no idea what you are *really* like. So it's important that you establish a good working relationship from the outset. Much of this will involve choosing the right words at the right time.

Once an employee has been with the company long enough, you will also need to deal with such things as performance reviews, raises, promotions, and firings. This is where your strength as a manager will really be tested, and where communicating clearly and confidently will count the most. Are you ready? Let's begin!

How to Speak to a New Employee

Effusive

- We're thrilled to have you on board. How can we make you feel at home?
- I can see that you're already fitting in just great.
- Soon you'll be just like one of the family.
- I don't know of anyone who has fit in so quickly!
- After a couple of hours you'll feel like an old timer, I promise.
- Great to have you working with us. Let me show you around.
- Don't worry. We'll show you the ropes until you feel more at home.
- It's okay to feel overwhelmed on your first day. You'll get over it.
- We all have to do our best to fit in here.
- Let's make this as painless as possible, okay?
- I'm sure you'll figure everything out on your own.
- I hope you're not one of those know-it-alls.
- If you have any questions, let me know. Otherwise, you're on your own.
- Try not to get yourself fired and you'll be fine.
- Just keep your head down and don't be a know-it-all.
- Well, you've certainly got a lot to learn.
- I like to throw the newbies into the deep end to see if they can swim. Don't take it personally.
- Oh great, another new hire.
- Let me see if there is anyone I can pawn you off to.
- You've got some big shoes to fill. I hope you're up for it.
- Even though you're new, try to at least act like you're interested.

- There's an office pool going to see how soon you get fired.
- Don't expect a lot of help from me.
- Honestly, I'd be surprised if you came back tomorrow.
- Who the heck hired *you*?

How to Give a Performance Review

Positive

- You should probably just run this company already.
- I have never been more comfortable reviewing anyone.
- You are the only person who could do this job, and do it so well.
- I expected nothing less from you, my star performer.
- You always over-deliver, and this time is no different.
- As always, another stellar performance review.
- I had to work really hard to find something negative to say.
- In general you did a good job, but there are a few areas that need improvement.
- You're competent. I'm not sure what else to say.
- Something is lacking in your performance.
- There is one little problem that you still need to address.
- Don't worry. I know you'll do better next time.
- When you are a vanilla performer, you get a vanilla review.

Negative

- Honestly, I'm on the fence about where you are headed in this company.
- I'm really not sure what to make of your performance this year. It's been so inconsistent.
- You're usually so on the ball. What happened?
- I have concerns about the overall trajectory of your work here.
- You used to be a diamond in the rough, but now there's more "rough" than "diamond."
- Honestly, I'm no longer sure you have what it takes.
- There are so many issues with your performance, I don't know what to address first.
- The math is simple: Poor performance equals poor review.
- I'm no longer sure you fit in here.
- If things don't get better fast, you'll be out by this time next year.
- If you don't get a grip, you'll be out by this time tomorrow.
- Once upon a time there was a good employee. But this story doesn't have a happy ending.
- At least you're consistent. You always let me down.

When an Employee Wants to Make a Lateral Move

Accepting

- They will be lucky to have you!
- They don't know how good they'll have it.
- I hear they're already cooling the champagne in advance of your arrival.
- Well, you won't get that promotion languishing over here.

- Good things come to those who wait, and your time has come.
- You're the most qualified person for that job.
- Of course I'll accommodate your request.
- If I were in your place I would want to move over there, too.
- I waited a long time to change jobs. Don't make the same mistake.
- What's taken you so long?
- No guts, no glory.
- If you weren't ready to take that on, I would tell you.
- I guess that's okay, but we'll miss you over here.
- I know how things work over there. Are you sure you're ready?
- You'd probably be better off staying where you are.
- Well, nobody's stopping you....
- It's the same pay with the same level of responsibility. So why do it?
- I'm not sure I can see you filling that position, but you're welcome to try.
- Knock yourself out, but don't come running back here when you fail.
- I wish you all the best, but I suspect you'll be back.
- I think you have a snowball's chance in hell of making this work.
- I can't believe you would abandon us like that.
- Out of the frying pan, into the fire.
- Lateral moves are for losers.
- So this is the thanks I get for hiring/training/ mentoring you?

Rejecting

When an Employee Asks for a Deserved Raise

Enthusiastic

- Is there anything else you want? A company car? Parking space?
- I think you deserve much more than that.
- I can't think of a more deserving employee.
- There's no one who deserves this more than you.
- Well, what's taken you so long to ask?
- You should have requested a raise a long time ago.
- I will do what I can for you, but I can't promise anything.
- I like your initiative, but I can't promise any more money than what you're asking.
- Okay, but don't let me down come crunch-time.
- You know this is going to require you to work even harder, right?
- Even with a raise, you're still one of our best bargains.
- Okay, but don't expect another raise come Christmas.
- Most employees wait a bit longer before asking for a raise.
- I guess so, but I'm not entirely enthusiastic about it.
- Tell me why we should give you a raise again?
- If we gave a raise to you, we'd have to elevate every other slacker that works here.
- I never thought we'd be giving raises to people like you.
- I'd better get my own raise request in first.
- Huh, you must know where all the bodies are buried.
- Who did you sleep with?

Begrudging

When an Employee Asks for a Undeserved Raise

Polite

- Once you're a little more seasoned and successful, I will consider what you're asking.
- I think you might have to wait a little longer.
- I know you have it in you, but you'll need to work a little harder.
- I can see why you would want more money, but it's just not in the cards right now.
- You want my advice? Improve your game and revisit this raise thing in six months.
- You'll need to straighten up and fly right if you want to be considered for a raise.
- I'll pretend you never asked, if you pretend you never saw the shocked disbelief on my face.
- You really don't understand how little a company values you until you ask for a raise.
- I have to admit that I admire your chutzpah.
- Unless you can guarantee me a ROI, I can't rationalize giving you a raise.
- I think I'll put this request in the circular file for now.
- Just because you ask for something doesn't mean you'll get it.
- Okay, tell me this: What have you done for us lately?
- Usually, people who ask for raises actually deserve them.
- Do you realize how ludicrous this request is, coming from you?
- Are you sure you want to ask me for this now?
- Perhaps if hell freezes over.
- You're the last person here I would offer a raise.
- All I have to say to you is *dream on.*

Blunt

- Forget about it.
- If I were to give you a raise, I think my staff would mutiny.
- Why should I reward shoddy performance?
- You can definitely get a raise—just not here.

How to Promote an Employee

Enthusiastic

- There is no one more worthy of a promotion.
- I'm surprised I had to wait this long to promote you, you're that good.
- With such stellar work, of course we had to promote you.
- I am certain you will continue to do great things for us.
- This is the least we could do, given your performance.
- By tomorrow you'll be one step closer to the corner office.
- It is my honor to promote you to [position/title].
- I just wish we could have done this for you sooner.
- I am investing in you by doing this. Please make me proud.
- I see great potential in promoting you, but there is some risk, too.
- I see no reason to deny you this promotion.
- Well, the spot was open and we couldn't think of anyone else.
- Now, don't let this go to your head.
- Just don't blow it.
- I'm very ambivalent about this. I hope you can cut the mustard.

Begrudging

- I'm only doing this because HR mandated it.
- I'm doing this against my better judgment.
- I guess you'll get to practice your unique brand of ineptness in someone else's department, now.
- I'm happy to promote you because I know it'll get you out of my sight.
- Do the phrases "backstabbing weasel" or "ass-kissing idiot" have anything to do with this?

How to Demote an Employee

Tactful

- If you are able to accept this with calmness and equanimity, I see great potential in you.
- Nobody likes to deliver bad news, but I can't think of any way to sweeten this.
- There's nothing like a challenge to forge character. This is just such a challenge.
- I really like you, so this is doubly hard for me to do.
- You have such potential, it pains me to have to do this.
- I know this is hard, but someday you will thank me for the lesson learned.
- This of this as an opportunity to regain our trust and hopefully make a new start.
- I hope you will be able to regroup and stay with us for the long haul.
- Sometimes we all need a wakeup call.
- There's no shame in taking more time to nurture your basic skills.
- My advice? Make the most of this new journey; you never know where it will take you.

- It's not a step backward; it's a step toward your future, this time on firmer footing.
- Part of being great is being able to keep going after setbacks.
- Very few people enjoy an uninterrupted ride to the top.
- I hate to have to do this, but...
- Don't you know this was difficult for me, too?
- We're reducing your responsibilities in the hopes that you can get your act together.
- I think this will be whatever you make of it. It's up to you.
- Show us what you can do, and in six months we'll talk again.
- It's just not working out here. We'll both be better off this way.
- You've really given me no choice, given your shoddy performance.
- You really should have seen this coming.
- Did you not see the handwriting on the wall?
- Would you prefer I fire you?
- The next step is termination, so consider this a final warning.

Blunt

How to Fire Someone

Empathic

- I feel terrible, but I am going to have to let you go.
- There is no easy way to say "you're fired," but hopefully the severance will help.
- I hate this part of my job, but I just don't think it's working out.
- It's difficult to for me to say this, and even more difficult for you to hear, I'm sure.
- Let me know if I can help your job search in any way.
- I am very sorry, but this is no longer working out.
- I regret to inform you that we have to let you go.
- Please do not take this personally. It was a business decision.
- I think it's best if we both go our separate ways.
- Management has determined that you no longer have a place here.
- I have no choice but to terminate you.
- There is no reason to sugarcoat this: You're fired.
- Hiring you was one of our biggest mistakes.
- It's probably best if you just left the premises right now.
- It appears that you've overstayed your welcome.
- I'm surprised no one fired you sooner.
- You're outta here.
- Two words: get out.

Blunt

When an Employee Quits

Conciliatory

- Please don't leave! You're irreplaceable.
- Is there anything I can say or do that will make you stay?
- I understand your reasons, but I'm very sorry to see you go.
- How will we ever replace you?
- I'm not sure what we're going to do without you.
- I really hope we can find someone to replace you.
- I truly wish you well in all your future endeavors.
- I feel terrible that it didn't work out.
- This is not how I envisioned this working out.
- Oh well, at least we tried.
- I was kind of expecting this, actually.
- Forgive me. I don't take this news too well.
- We'll adjust without you, I'm sure.
- No worries. It's not like you're irreplaceable.
- We'll find someone as good as if not better than you, I'm sure.
- Honestly, I think we're both better off this way.
- Good luck to you. You're gonna need it.
- I never knew what I'd say when this happened, but now I do: "Take a hike."
- It's your funeral.
- Don't let the door hit you on the way out.
- We actually began training your replacement a month ago.
- You just made my day.

Punitive

When an Employee Wants Time Off

Amenable

- Please take as much time as you need.
- Of course—you deserve it.
- We all need to take time off once in a while. Sure, you can go.
- I don't see any problem with that.
- I guess that's okay. How much time were you needing?
- There's no reason you shouldn't ask, and no reason I shouldn't grant it.
- Well, do what you think is best.
- Do you really think that's the best idea right now?
- We'd all like a little time off, but do you think that's a good idea?
- It's just not possible at the moment, I'm afraid.
- We all need to buckle down and think realistically during these tough times.
- If it were up to me, I would give you all the time you needed—but it's not.
- I wish I could help you out, but times are tough right now.
- I feel your pain, but this is one of those times you need to take one for the team.
- When the rest of us are able to take a break, so will you.
- If I were to give you time off, I'd have to give it to everyone else, too.
- Sorry, this is crunch time; you'll have plenty of time to take off later.
- I was counting on you to be here.
- I'm going to have to deny your time off request.

Unwilling

- Your personal desires don't take precedence here.
- Give me one good reason why I should grant you this request.
- We'll have to revisit this another time.
- There's nothing that could convince me to say yes.
- If I gave you a vacation right now, I'd have to make it permanent.
- There's no way I'm granting you vacation time. You need to earn it first.
- You'll have to pry your vacation approval from my cold, dead fingers.
- I am not about to jeopardize this company simply because you need your beauty rest.
- Hell no.

Part 2
Ethics and Legalities

Judgment comes through experience; experience comes through bad judgment.
—Unknown

It can be reassuring to have so many clear-cut rules and regulations governing how businesses are run these days. For example, knowing that you cannot physically abuse your reports—nor can they abuse you—is a very clear cut line that should never be crossed from either direction. But we all know that people don't always observe the rules. They think the rules don't apply to them or that they are somehow above the law. If this describes you, you clearly have a problem that is bigger than just you and your department!

Fortunately, chances are you're an honest sort who wants to do the right thing. But even with all those rules, it's not always easy. Anyone who has ever studied law or ethics will tell you that the ways in which the rules can or ought to be applied is not always clear-cut. So naturally, it's usually best to vet any legal or ethical issues with HR and, if necessary, in-house counsel before you respond to the situation at hand. Once you know what you're dealing with, check out the phrases in this section. They may just help you communicate more effectively in these difficult situations.

When an Employee Violates Safety Regulations

Lenient

- Everyone slips up now and then; just be more careful next time.
- I'm sure it was an honest mistake. Let's go over the safety rules again.
- Just make sure you never do that again.
- Everyone cuts corners occasionally, but getting caught will get us both fired.
- I would feel terrible if you got injured.
- What's the point of taking those kinds of risks?
- Safety is everyone's priority, and that includes you, too.
- Remember what they said in kindergarten? Safety first.
- It's everyone's responsibility to stay safe, and you need to understand that.
- I didn't make the safety guidelines, but we all need to abide by them.
- You've endangered everyone here, not just yourself. Remember that.
- I'll let this pass this one time, but don't let it happen again.
- One more violation and I'll have to report you.
- It's pretty simple: Be safe on the job or be prepared to face the consequences.
- You've left me no choice but to put you on probation/demote you/fire you.
- Other people have been lax about safety, sure, but they're no longer with the company.
- We have a two-strike policy here; it happens again and you're fired.
- I don't give a damn about you. It's my company that you are putting at risk.

Stringent

- There's simply no place in this company for someone who flaunts the basic rules of safety.
- You are perhaps the sloppiest employee I've ever encountered.
- There may be more egregious mistakes, but I can't think of any at the moment.
- Some people don't think safety is important. Some of those people are dead now.
- Yes, you are fired, but be grateful you aren't dead.
- I have to fire you before you get yourself or someone else killed.
- If you like to play with danger so much, maybe you should go jump off a cliff.

When an Employee Abuses the Company Credit Card/Expense Account

Lax

- I'm sure you didn't mean any harm. Did you at least get anything good?
- Everyone does it at some point; just don't let it happen again.
- I'm sure it was just a misunderstanding. Let's review the policy again.
- Slip-ups are understandable; just watch yourself in the future.
- I'm sure that was an honest slip. At least I'm assuming it was.
- We need to figure this out before the higher-ups get wind of it.
- I was just reviewing your expense report and there are a few red flags I want to go over.
- Did you get the company card mixed up with your personal card or something?

Punitive

- There are holes in your expense report big enough to drive a truck through.
- No one else on the trip had these kinds of expenditures. How can you justify this?
- About half of the items you expensed are questionable. If you can't rein it in, we'll have to pursue the matter from a higher level.
- Some people around here turn a blind eye to oddities on the credit statement, but not me.
- This kind of petty theft won't wash here.
- This is a serious matter that I cannot let slide.
- I never pegged you for a thief.
- I believe this amounts to "Grand Theft Expense Account."
- No one can take advantage of us like that.
- In all my years of working here, this is the most extreme case of expense report padding I've ever seen.
- Please turn in your company credit card. And while you're at it, bring your ID card, too. You're fired.

When an Employee Lies

Lax

- We all tell little white lies from time to time.
- I'm sure you meant no harm by your statement.
- If I didn't know you better, I'd say your pants were on fire. [joking]
- Who am I to point a bony finger at you?
- Everyone steps in it from time to time. Best not to make it a habit, though.

- I'm going to let you restate that, because I know I didn't hear you right.
- It doesn't look like you have your facts straight. Perhaps there's been a misunderstanding?
- Between you and me, your statement just doesn't feel right.
- We have an honesty policy here, so perhaps you should rethink what you just said.
- Telling lies will never get you where you want to go.
- No one has ever lied their way to the top and stayed there for long.
- When you start lying, the problem is that you never know when to stop.
- It would be best to think first next time.
- People who lie completely lose my respect.
- What you said just doesn't add up.
- There is no way that can be true.
- I have never heard anything so preposterous in my life.
- Do you simply lack the capacity to be truthful?
- Oh what a tangled web we weave, when first we practice to deceive.
- You're not a very good liar, you know.
- Lie to me twice? Shame on me!
- If you continue running your mouth, I'll run you out of town.
- You have no idea just how damaging your words are.
- Methinks your tongue is forked.
- I come from a long line of liars; it takes one to know one.
- How can I tell you're lying? You lips are moving.

Punitive

When an Employee Steals

Circuitous

- I did the accounting this morning and came up a little short. There must be some mistake.
- You haven't seen that missing money/item by chance, have you?
- Do you know anything about the missing money/merchandise/supplies?
- If you have any information about the missing funds, we would appreciate it.
- If you have something that belongs to us, you can give it back now, no questions asked.
- If you took the money, it would be better if you came forward of your own accord.
- There is only a small window in which the missing money can be returned without penalty. I would recommend it.
- We are showing a significant loss. What do you know about this?
- I don't know who did this, but I'll figure it out.
- Your story has too many holes to be credible.
- I can't say that we caught you red-handed, but you were the only person with access and motive.
- We never had a theft like this until you showed up.
- The only problem with your story is that you didn't count on witnesses.
- When I reach for my wallet, it seems that your hand is already there.
- I believe you have something that we want, yes?
- I know you're the guilty party. Just fess up.
- You had motive, opportunity, and means.

Direct

- Drop the stolen goods, then leave before I call the police.
- I'm calling the police.
- You're fired, and we'll see you in court.

When an Employee Steals Someone's Idea

Subtle

- Describe to me how you came up with this idea. It's really good!
- This seems remarkably similar to so-and-so's idea. That sure seems like a coincidence!
- I could be wrong, but didn't I see something else like this recently?
- I've seen all of this before and unfortunately it was on your associate's drawing board.
- I was once tempted to use someone else's idea, but then I realized that it was basically stealing.
- While I wouldn't call this out-and-out thievery, it basically is, if you think about it.
- You do realize that this violates almost all the tenets of intellectual property, don't you?
- I think that any competent copyright attorney could help you see the error of your ways.
- I have no respect for people who steal the ideas of others.
- We see this kind of thing all the time, and it won't garner you any praise here.
- I'm surprised that you would stoop this low, given your intelligence and originality.
- You don't have a single original idea in your head, do you?
- Only a coward would steal so outrageously.

Overt

- There is no excuse for stealing.
- You would copy your mother's own recipe for apple pie.
- If you're okay with ripping off other people, who knows what you'll be capable of in the future?
- You know what happens to thieves and plagiarists, don't you? They get fired.

When an Employee Leaks Confidential Information

Lenient

- I'm sure it was an accident, but please be more careful next time.
- What you divulged was relatively trivial, thank goodness.
- It's so easy to forget how critical this kind of information is; next time you'll know better, I'm sure.
- We would never be able to stay in business if all our secrets were given away; I hope you understand that.
- No one has the right to leak confidential information.
- Everyone suffers when someone can't withhold confidential information.
- A simple slip of the lip can ruin everything. You really need more control over your tongue.
- Company secrets are called "secrets" for a reason. How can you not get that?
- It isn't my place to judge you, but you really need to straighten up and fly right.
- We have rules about this, and there are stiff penalties for those who can't follow the rules.

- Confidentiality is everyone's business, even yours.
- Keeping our company's secrets safe is Job One for everyone.
- When did it ever become a good thing to sell us out to a competitor?
- Your failure to protect our information is inexcusable.
- You've betrayed us. How can we not take that personally?
- You sold out me *and* your fellow employees. How does that feel?
- I never pegged you for a spy or, worse, a Quisling.
- People who can't keep their mouths closed have a way of leaving here rather quickly.
- There is only one word that fits you: Blabbermouth.
- If you can't keep your lip zipped, you can't work here.
- By leaking secret information, you've crossed the line.
- Apparently you never learned how to keep your mouth shut.

Punitive

When an Employee Is Sexually Harassing Someone

Lenient

- I'm sure you didn't mean to be offensive, but just think of it from the other person's point of view.
- Although I know your motives were pure, you're going to need to watch that going forward.
- That may have been tolerated in other companies you've worked for, but not by us.
- Some of this behavior is pathological. You really should get some help.
- No one can be allowed to continue doing what you're doing—not you, not me, not anyone.
- Using sexual innuendo around an employee isn't helping you here. You should stop doing it right away.
- There is no excuse for acting in an inappropriate way, especially in light of our sexual harassment training.
- Your inability to control yourself is going to land you in hot water.
- We have policies against sexual harassment here, but they do no good if they're ignored.
- I would like to discuss your inappropriate behavior with you in private.
- Once you cross the line it will be too late. You really need to rein yourself in.
- I'll let this go this one time, but next time there will likely be consequences.
- Behavior like yours can't be tolerated, but I don't see myself being the whistleblower.
- God knows I'm not perfect, either, but we need some sense of order around here.

Punitive

- You're only putting a noose around your own neck. Cut it out.
- Just keep doing what you're doing and you'll get what you get.
- Forewarned is forearmed. Ignore this warning at your peril.
- It's a wonder you've gotten this far. Watch yourself.
- I never realized you were such a creep.
- There is no place around here for a louse like you. Get help or get out.
- Your behavior sickens me, and I'm sure it makes other people sick, too.
- You're obviously compensating for your low self-esteem; perhaps some counseling would help.
- Your behavior can get us both fired. Stop it right now or I'll blow the whistle on you.
- Clearly you have no morals. You're fired.

When an Employee Is Bullying or Threatening Someone

Lenient

- You seem really angry. Is there something I can do to help?
- We all need to vent from time to timel; tell me what's going on.
- Everyone gets a little hot under the collar some-times, but we can't tolerate bullying or threats.
- I agree that this person can be frustrating, but you can't let it get to you.
- You have the right to your feelings, just not the right to express them the way that you have been.

- This is a no-bullying zone. I hope you understand that.
- There is no stigma in being a bully if you simply admit that you need help.
- Self-control is a necessary attribute in all of my employees, including you.
- I know some anger management classes that could help you.
- I think you should seek out professional help to get your behavior under control.
- Bully tactics aren't tolerated here. You need to check yourself.
- I don't care how mad you are; you can't go around acting like that. Period.
- We would be happy to get you some professional help under strict confidentiality.
- I used to bully people, too–when I was in grammar school.
- Keep it up and someone is going to put you in your place.
- No one likes or respects a bully–or didn't you get that memo?
- If acting out were an Olympic sport, you'd take the gold medal.
- The solution is really simple: Cut it out, or you're fired.
- I once knew a guy who couldn't control his temper. He may or may not still be in jail.
- What happened to you that you are such a sadist?
- Did someone drop you on your head when you were a baby?
- There is no place here for an infantile bully like you. Pack your things and get out.

Punitive

When an Employee Is Injured at Work

Concerned

- Your health and safety are my primary concerns; the work is secondary.
- You're hurt. Don't even think of coming back to work!
- Please take the rest of the day off and see a doctor.
- I feel terrible you got hurt. Can I help in any way?
- I once had an experience like that. How are you doing?
- From where I was sitting that looked serious. Do you need a ride home?
- You should rest up and take care of yourself until you are better.
- That looks serious. You'd better get it seen to right away.
- Don't worry, I'll have someone else take over for a while.
- Are you sure you can continue? Maybe you should sit it out for a spell.
- Don't be a hero; make sure you're okay before you dive back in, okay?
- When do you think you'll be able to come back? I'm just concerned about your workload.
- I know you think you're okay, but I don't want any lawsuits down the road.
- It's your decision. Do whatever you're most comfortable with.
- You *could* take a little more time if you wanted, but do what you think is best.
- If you think you need some time off, feel free to speak to the folks in HR.
- As they say, the show must go on.

Dismissive

- We really need to finish up today. What would you recommend?
- Please get back to work as soon as you can; we're under the gun here.
- Well, no one likes a malingerer, but do what you think is best.
- This has never happened here before; I get the feeling you did it on purpose.
- You don't expect me to let you off after every little scrape, do you?
- If I'd known you were such a baby, I would never have hired you in the first place.

When an Employee Uses the Internet Unadvisedly

Lenient

- Everyone surfs the Web at work, but it needs to be within reasonable limits.
- Just FYI: It's okay to check Facebook once in a while, but not throughout the entire day.
- The Internet has had a negative effect on productivity, so we're taking it away from everyone.
- Now I understand why your work has been suffering so much lately. What can we do about this?
- While a little bit of Web surfing goes with the territory, you're overstepping the boundaries.
- Please confine your Web browsing to work-related activities.
- You could be a lot more productive with a lot less surfing on the Web.
- Some employees set a timer to tell them when their online time is over.

- People who can't stop surfing are usually addicted–but that isn't you, is it?
- The only shame in this is in not admitting you need help.
- IT sent me your surfing report and I was pretty shocked.
- Look, it's definitely a problem, but the solution is fairly simple: Just knock it off.
- Since when is this a part of your job description?
- Wow! You certainly enjoy social media, don't you? [*sarcastic*]
- If it happens again, I'll make sure your Web privileges are suspended.
- Don't think for a minute that we can't tell what you're doing.
- Not a threat, but the last person who assumed he was above the rules is now pumping gas.
- Get it under control or your job will be in jeopardy.
- Seems like you might have an internet addiction. Ever thought of getting some counseling?
- If you can't concentrate on your work, you'll need to work for someone else.

Strict

Part 3
Feedback and Discipline

There are three classes of people: those who see, those who see when they are shown, and those who do not see.
—Leonardo Da Vinci

Let's be honest—you probably tend to come down on one of two sides when it comes to this aspect of your job: You either love it or you hate it! You're either a results-oriented taskmaster who loves to wield control (either subtly or overtly), or you're a kind-hearted idealist who wants to encourage and inspire at every turn. Might there be a more comfortable middle ground available to you, as well? The good news is that there is. You don't need to sacrifice your authority and power to motivate your employees and treat them like human beings, nor do you have to act like a dictator to keep order and achieve results.

That said, there is a time for everything. Sometimes you will be required to lower the boom on someone who is really taking advantage, and sometimes you will need to soften your approach when you are dealing with a fragile person.

Read on to find out how to strike the perfect balance each and every time.

How to Open a Difficult Conversation

Conciliatory

- I'm glad we can talk to each other so openly. By the way, do you have a moment? There are a few things I need to get off my chest.

- It's always good to be able to bounce things off of other people.

- I can't remember the last time we had a good chat; is this a good time for you?

- Is this a good time to talk? There are a few things I want to go over with you.

- I know it's hard to talk to your boss about stuff, but just think of me as a friend.

- There's something that's been bothering me that I would like your input on.

- This is a difficult conversation for me, so please bear with me as I gather my thoughts.

- I need to speak with you about something; please feel free to speak your mind, as well.

- I think we need to talk. Please get back to me with a time that is convenient for you.

- I think it's best if we just speak frankly to one another. Wouldn't you agree?

- I'm at a loss as to what to do about this. Perhaps you have some ideas?

- We have a problem, and you're going to need to suggest some solutions.

- You obviously have a problem, and I'd like *you* to tell me what you think it is.

- We all need to have difficult conversations at some point, and this is one of those times.

- Can I have a word with you in private? We need to talk.

- It's critical that we talk about something ASAP.

Blunt

- I think we have a problem. Please step into my office.
- I'm just going to come out and say it: We need to talk. *Now.*
- In my office, five minutes.
- I am going to talk, and you are going to listen, okay?

How to Express a Specific Concern

Polite

- Forgive me, but could we discuss this further? I just want to put my mind at rest.
- There's just one thing that's bothering me about this....
- I have a concern that I would like to voice, if that is okay with you/everyone.
- I do have some reservations. When can we talk about this?
- This gives me pause, and here is why....
- You know, it seems like there could be a potential problem here.
- No one seems to want to talk about this, but I think we need to.
- Nobody here should feel afraid to voice their concerns. For example...
- Let's revisit this for a moment. I'm sure I'm not the only one with doubts.
- I'd like to put everything out on the table, okay?
- Ignoring a problem will only make it worse, don't you agree?

Rude

- I think we need to look at this issue objectively and rationally.
- The unanimity has me a bit concerned: Where are the dissenting voices?
- I think we need to discuss this until everyone's concerns are resolved.
- I think we need to face reality: This is a problem.
- Can we at least agree that there *is* a problem?
- Am I the only person who is concerned?
- May I ask you *why* you think this is okay?
- Did you really have no idea that this could be problematic?
- There are none so blind as those who refuse to see.
- This is crazy!

How to Give Unsolicited Advice

Gentle

- May I offer my opinion? I don't want to step on anyone's toes.
- I know I tend to stick my nose into places when I don't need to. [*joking*]
- I know nobody asked, but I'd like to weigh on this if that's okay.
- Advice is worth about what you pay for it, but hope that you'd at least consider my input.
- Perhaps you'd like to hear my perspective on the situation?
- You look like you could use a sounding board. Is that true?

- Have you considered asking a neutral outsider for his opinion?
- I know you're not in the mood to listen to advice right now, but please hear me out.
- I can understand why you wouldn't want to hear this, but I simply cannot remain silent.
- No one wants to receive unsolicited input, but I'd be remiss if I didn't say anything.
- No one is asking me to get involved, but I can't keep quiet any longer.
- Everyone needs help now and then; don't be too proud to ask for it.
- There is wisdom in the counsel of many.
- No man is an island, and this is doubly true for you.
- You obviously need help, and I'm just the person for the job.
- You'll regret it if you don't listen to what I have to say.
- You're clearly not ready to listen, but I'm going to tell you what I think anyway.
- I think you'll regret it if you don't at least consider my opinion.
- You discount the opinions of others at your peril.
- So, since when do you know everything?

Directive

How to Address Underperformance

Delicate

- I've noticed that you're having a tough time at work. Is there any way I can help?
- You seem a bit out of your depth lately. Are you having trouble with something specific?
- You seem a bit, well, off your game lately. Is something wrong?
- There's a lot more to you than what I've been seeing lately. What gives?
- You seem to be floundering a bit lately. What's going on?
- You are letting your teammates down. Did you know that?
- I know I've certainly gone through dry spells at work. How are you doing?
- Your work has been slipping lately. Is there something wrong?
- You don't seem to have your act together. What's going on?
- Your underperforming is cheating everyone, not just yourself.
- We need to discuss your underperformance. What's the story?
- You've been underperforming, and we need to address it before it becomes a problem.
- The higher-ups have been noticing your lack of productivity.
- You may not care how your performance is affecting others, but I do.
- We all depend on one another here, but you're no longer doing your part.
- Everyone has been contributing here lately except you.

Blunt

- A company can't survive constantly covering for a worker who is a dead weight.
- If I were you, I'd be worried about keeping my job at this point.
- If you don't shape up, you'll need to ship out, I'm afraid.
- It's really simple: You either fix this or you're fired.

How to Ask to Speak With an Employee Privately

Delicate

- Whenever I need to have a serious discussion, it just makes sense to do it in private.
- When you have a moment, I'd like to have a word with you in private.
- I like to play my cards close to my chest. Let's take this somewhere private.
- This is the kind of discussion that is best had behind closed doors.
- We really need to keep this *entre nous*, okay?
- There is something of some importance I need to speak with you about in private.
- Let's discuss this in a room/office where we can have some privacy.
- Can we talk—I mean in private?
- I think it's best that we meet away from prying eyes and ears.
- There's no sense in blabbing about this in front of everyone, right?
- Some things are just better kept confidential.

Blunt

- I need to speak briefly with you in private.
- I must have a private word with you about something.
- Confidentiality is important when discussing matters such as these.
- Unless you're interested in broadcasting this to the world, let's meet in private.
- The only way I will discuss this with you is behind closed doors.
- Loose lips sink ships.

How to Provide Constructive Criticism

Gentle

- Please don't take this the wrong way, but I see room for improvement.
- Your work here is very good overall, but I think you can bring it to an even higher level.
- Let's start this off on a positive note. Here's what you are doing well....
- Nobody's perfect, although you're pretty close!
- I know you are capable of great things here, if you just tie up these loose ends.
- You're a great employee, but there is always room for improvement, right?
- I hope you will take this in the spirit in which it was intended—with caring for you as an employee—and a person.
- I appreciate getting honest feedback on my work, so I want to provide that to you, too.
- I know it's difficult to receive feedback, but the benefits far outweigh the temporary discomfort.

Blunt

- Are you open to feedback? I want to have your buy-in on the front end.
- To profit from feedback, you need to be open to it; are you?
- Most people don't like criticism, but you'll need to get used to it if you want to do well here.
- Everyone benefits from being critiqued, even you.
- No one is perfect, and you're no exception.
- I'm just going to be blunt here and tell you where you really need to improve.
- Let's face it: Your performance in this particular area has been sorely lacking.
- I have serious concerns about your performance. What do you plan on doing to correct this?
- I'd like to help you, but I don't even know where to start.
- How long will the critique session last? Well, how much time you have?

How to Discipline or Punish a Valued Employee

Empathic

- I think we can look at this as an opportunity for growth and learning.
- It's when we fail and make mistakes that we grow the most.
- I hate this part of my job, but I would be remiss if I didn't address this.
- It pains me to do this, but you are *worth* disciplining.

- If you weren't such a valuable employee, I wouldn't even bother discussing this.
- If I didn't set an example by punishing you, there would be chaos here.
- This will hurt me more than it hurts you.
- I look forward to seeing you learn and grow from this challenge.
- I certainly never thought I'd be sitting here with *you*.
- We all make mistakes, me included, and you are no different.
- Anyone can take a wrong turn, so I'll just let you off with a warning.
- You've always been a good worker, but this wrong must be righted.
- I hate to have to do this, but...
- Clean up your act and I'm sure it won't happen again.
- The punishment must fit the crime.
- There's no way around it, I'm afraid.
- What do *you* think would be fair? You know, since you're the one who messed up.
- Given the magnitude of what transpired, I have to impose some kind of penalty.
- You made a mistake and unfortunately you will need to pay.
- The future is up to you. I hope you handle this in the right way.
- You're digging your own hole here.
- Disciplining employees is not something I enjoy, but you deserve it this time.
- Consider this a learning experience—one that you ignore at your peril.

Harsh

- Unfortunately I'm going to have to take you down a peg or two.
- I'm going to need to lower the boom on you.
- You screwed up, so you're the one who will have to absorb the cost.
- One more of these incidents and I'll have to re-think your employment here.

How to Express Disappointment

Kind

- I am disappointed, but I know you will make things right.
- Sure, I feel let down, but I'm more interested in how *you* feel about this.
- Yes, this is tough, but let's think of this as a fresh start, okay?
- If I feel let down it's because I have such high re-gard for you.
- I feel that I have failed you by not addressing this sooner.
- Despite my disappointment, I have every reason to believe that you will make this right.
- Although I am disappointed, I know you will do better next time.
- We all disappoint others from time to time. I'll get over it.
- Yes, I feel let down, but there are things you can do to make it right.
- You always over-deliver; what happened this time?
- You've got to fly straight or else you'll crash on landing.
- You're going to have to figure out how to get back into my good graces.

Harsh

- You let me down, and honestly I'm not sure what you can do to make it right.
- Honestly I'm not sure what kind of compensation would be enough.
- I'm not sure if there is a path to redemption, after what you've done.
- I'm so disappointed, I don't even know what to say to you.
- What do you have to say for yourself?
- There is simply no excuse for what you've done, here.
- Maybe it's time you found someone else to disappoint.

How to Express Anger

Restrained

- My emotions should not be our focus right now.
- Although I am upset and angry, that's not what I want to focus on.
- Yes, I am angry, but the main thing is that we find a solution.
- Although I am angry, indulging my feelings and expressing them will get us nowhere.
- While I am angry, I don't think it's productive to address that right now.
- Instead of getting angry, I'm going to count to 10 and try to calm down.
- I'm not gonna lie: I'm pretty pissed right now.
- I'm right on the verge of losing it. Can't you see that?

Demonstrative

- I think we need to take a timeout and return to this when we can both discuss things rationally.
- You are fortunate that I have such self-control.
- You can't negotiate emotions, you know!
- I have every right to be upset right now!
- I admit it: I'm angry.
- Do I *look* like I'm happy right now? [*sarcasm*]
- I'm so angry at you, I don't even know *what* to say to you anymore!
- If you are interested in saving your hide, you'd better have your desk cleaned out by the time I get back.
- I have nothing but contempt for you right now.
- I'm trying figure out why I shouldn't tear you a new one right now.

Machiavellian Tactics

Covert

- I've got your best interests at heart; you can count on me.
- We think of this place as one big family.
- Loyalty is really the most important thing here.
- If we can't trust one another, what do we have?
- Trust me, I am looking out for your best interest.
- You shouldn't trust anyone around here.
- Don't you trust us?
- If you say so.
- So you say.
- Really?

- Is that true?
- I would have expected better from you.
- Huh—I thought you knew better than that.
- Are you really sure you want to do that?
- Can't you see I'm just trying to help you?
- Are you saying that I'm *not* on your side?
- I think you may the one with the issues here.
- I'm not saying you *shouldn't* be worried.
- If I didn't care, we wouldn't be having this conversation.
- I'm just trying to help you understand how it is around here.
- Things would go a lot more smoothly for you here if you just took my advice.
- You do what you do, you get what you get.
- You reap what you sow, is all I'm saying.
- You can't make an omelet without breaking some eggs.
- Just think of it as collateral damage.
- I'm just saying to not be surprised when you see how things turn out.
- Trust me, you don't want to go that route.
- Things will not go well for you if that's your final decision.
- I think you should think long and hard before moving forward.
- It's not a good idea to get on anyone's bad side here.
- Don't make me angry. You wouldn't like me when I'm angry.
- That wouldn't be a very healthy choice for you right now.

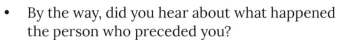

- By the way, did you hear about what happened the person who preceded you?
- I'm not sure what your problem is, given how much we do for you here.
- After all I've done for you?
- Forewarned is forearmed: I'm an equal opportunity bastard.
- Now that you see what I've done for you, how are you going to help *me*?
- After all we've done for your career, you owe us.

Overt

Part 4
Bad Behavior

Every saint has a past; every sinner has a future.
–Oscar Wilde

Human beings are pretty much the same everywhere you go. Unless you are dealing with a sociopath, most people have their good and their bad sides (yes, that goes for you, too!). This means that you'll need to be prepared for bad behavior from your direct reports every now and then. It's important to not be shocked when these things inevitably occur. But it's also important not to assume that everyone is out to get you or bilk the company for all it's worth. I think "enlightened realism" is the best approach.

If you want to be cynical, I won't stop you–but know the toll that this will take on your employees and on the company as a whole. If you don't trust them, why should they trust you? Conversely, naiveté is not the way to go, either. Just think of Ronald Reagan's pet phrase: "Trust, but verify." Start from a place of trust, but be cognizant that you are dealing with human beings, always.

When an Employee Is Perpetually Late

Caring/Concerned

- Your constant lateness has me a bit worried. Is everything okay?
- When you're late, everyone worries that you're lying in a ditch somewhere.
- I understand that getting here is a hassle, but we all have to deal with it.
- I just can't accept this tardiness from someone who has so much potential.
- What can we do to help you get here on time every day?
- Let's work together to hash out a plan to get you here on time, okay?
- You seem to have difficulty getting here on time; how can we fix this?
- I don't think we need to let this become a problem, do you?
- You're not lazy, just mismanaged. I blame myself.
- We're all late from time to time, but in your case it's gotten out of hand.
- It's not fair to the other employees when you come in late each day.
- Make me look good by getting here on time each day, all right?
- Your tardiness has become a pattern and is even being noticed by the CEO.
- It's really simple: Just leave your house a little earlier in the morning.
- Your time will be valuable only if you value your time.
- Showing up—and showing up on time—is 90 percent of the job.

Overt/Rude

- If I showed up late as many times as you, I'd have been shown the door a long time ago.
- Most people who want to climb to the top climb out of bed a little earlier.
- Would you like me to buy you a new alarm clock? [*sarcasm*]
- I find that the bills I have to pay really help get me get to work on time. [*sarcasm*]
- Your perpetual lateness appears to be a pathological disorder; maybe you need help.
- If you are late again without a valid excuse, we'll have to put you on probation.
- The next time you waltz in late, I'll waltz over and serve you your walking papers.
- If I were you I'd be on time from now on—if you still want your job, that is.

When an Employee Exhibits Excessive Absenteeism

Subtle

- We're all very worried about you; is there anything I can do to help?
- I'm sure you have a valid reason for missing so much work. Let me know if I can do anything.
- I'm very concerned about the number of days you've been out. Is everything okay?
- I really hope you can get back on track with your schedule. We miss you and all that you do here.
- Ah, there you are; we'd almost forgotten what you looked like. [*joking*]
- I just can't stand by idly while you're missing so much work. What's going on?

Blunt

- Perhaps I should notify HR about this. They may be able to recommend some solutions.
- We really need to get to the bottom of why you're out so often.
- We can't afford to carry any dead weights, which is what is happening here.
- This company won't stop moving if one part is missing. Please keep that in mind.
- Your continual absence is really unfair to the people who actually show up and do the work.
- Calling in "sick" is like stealing money from our company.
- I think we're going to have to start looking into a responsible replacement for you.
- I think your department may have rented out your desk by now.
- Anyone who takes this many days off must be very sick, indeed.
- How kind of you to grace us with your presence today. [*sarcasm*]
- Don't bother coming back. We've found someone else.

When an Employee Exhibits Presenteeism

Compassionate

- You've obviously got a lot on your mind. Is it anything I can help you with?
- I understand you've been distracted, but this job requires all of your focus.
- You just don't seem "here" lately. Is everything okay?
- You're here, but it feels like your mind is elsewhere. What's going on?
- I'm concerned that you're not as invested in your work as you should be.
- I get the feeling that you're just a seat-warmer these days. Am I wrong?
- You seem to be marking time here lately. What's going on?
- Yes, showing up is 90 percent of the job, but you're ignoring the other 10 percent.
- I'd like you to start keeping a log of how you spend your time here.
- Your being here but not doing any work is tantamount to stealing money from the company.
- You're always here, but for some reason nothing ever gets done. Care to explain that?
- So we're basically paying you so that you can keep a chair warm?
- What is it that you do here, exactly? [sarcasm]

Rude

When an Employee Fails to Meet Goals/Deadlines

Conciliatory

- You seem really overwhelmed. What can I do to help?
- Have I put too much on your plate? Please tell me so I can help fix this.
- Let's talk about prioritizing tasks and how we can help you manage your time better.
- You're working hard, but nothing is getting done on time. How can we fix that?
- Everyone has occasional trouble meeting deadlines, but this is getting to be a problem.
- We've all had issues with time management, but this has become untenable.
- I know you're trying your best, but something's not working. What will you do to fix this?
- You probably don't realize how often your work is late, but I know others do.
- It *looks* like you're working, but when push comes to shove, you don't deliver.
- I think I'm going to need to monitor how you are using your time.
- Talent without time management is useless.
- It's really unfair to the others that they constantly have to cover for you.
- Most people who are unable to meet deadlines don't keep their jobs.
- It really isn't up to me to teach you how to use your time wisely.
- People who can't manage their time don't last long here.
- If this were a reality show, you would have already been voted off the island.

Harsh

- Every time you fail to deliver is just another nail in your coffin.
- How can you feel good about yourself, knowing how you let us down like this?
- Do you enjoy the sound of deadlines as they whoosh past you?
- If I were a betting man, I'd bet you were playing solitaire instead of working.
- When I say a project is due tomorrow, I don't mean the day after tomorrow.
- Perhaps you weren't there when punctuality and responsibility were covered in first grade.
- Will you even fail to show up on time for your exit interview?

When an Employee Spends Too Much Time Socializing

Understanding

- I'm really glad you enjoy your job, but I think it's time to be a little more focused.
- Everyone needs a social outlet, but work shouldn't be it.
- Everyone here obviously likes you, but I'm concerned about your work ethic.
- The social butterflies rarely get promoted. Just saying...
- Let's take care of business and then chat later, okay?
- You are such a great, fun person, but the work needs to come first.
- The social aspect of this job is important, but I think we need to rein it in a little.

- I see great things happening for you if you just concentrate on work.
- It's great that you all get along, but it's time to buckle down.
- My best workers have always been the ones who were least interested in socializing.
- I think we need a little less goofing off on the job, okay?
- I can tolerate a certain amount of idle chatter, but this is going overboard.
- I know it's important to get along with everyone, but it's also important to get the work done.
- I think we need to institute a "no socializing" policy from 8 a.m. until closing.
- Every minute you chat, you are stealing from this company.
- You can't complain about never getting anything done when all you do is gab.
- Please save all your interesting stories for your personal time.
- Your anecdotes are best served during happy hour.
- It's not fair for you to take up everyone's time with idle chatter.
- If I allowed this to continue, I'd be the one at fault.
- "Best Office Entertainer of the Year" is *not* a title you should aspire to.
- Someone at your level shouldn't need to be reminded to work.
- If I added up all the hours you actually worked, I could do it on one hand.
- People who waste time rarely make it here.

Strict

- I'm just going to come out and say it: Shut your trap and get back to work.
- Let me clue you in on something: No one here cares about your stupid stories.
- I don't know what we'd do without you here to entertain us. [*sarcasm*]

When an Employee Makes Too Many Personal Calls

Lax

- I make personal calls, too; just don't get caught doing it.
- We all need to make personal phone calls; just keep it reasonable, okay?
- I tend to make personal calls only if it's something really urgent or an emergency.
- We all want to know what's going on at home, but you need to rein it in a bit.
- I don't mind a few phone calls during work hours, but this is getting out of hand.
- There is a time and a place for personal calls, and this isn't it.
- It's best to limit your phone time to business matters only.
- It's one thing to make a personal call or two during the day, but what you're doing is unprofessional.
- Think of it this way: What if I spent all day on the phone? How would you feel?
- We have rules about personal calls at your desk. Maybe you should review them.
- Your making personal calls during office hours is really becoming an issue.

Strict

- If this doesn't change, we're going to have to institute some controls on your phone use.
- You need to work on keeping your personal life and work life separate.
- The amount of company time you spend on personal calls is way out of control.
- We're going to dock your pay for the amount of time you spend on the phone gabbing.
- We don't want to monitor everyone's personal calls, but you're forcing our hand.
- We are not paying you to chat on the phone, so knock it off.
- If you can't manage your personal phone calls, we'll need to revisit your employment here.
- You can make *all* the personal calls you want–from your home, after we fire you.

When an Employee Doesn't Play Well With Others

Encouraging

- We all need to row in the same direction.
- I think you'll be surprised at what you can achieve as part of a team.
- I know it's tough, but we all need to make an effort to play well with others.
- Together, all of us will achieve more.
- We all depend on one another to succeed.
- Can you at least meet the others halfway?
- I would really encourage you to collaborate more with your teammates.

- No one is an island here, so please try to work with your coworkers.
- We all need to make an effort to get along with one another.
- A big part of our success here is being able to work as part of a team. Can you do that?
- Coworkers can sometimes bring out the worst in you, but the onus is on you to make it work.
- You are so talented, yet so unenlightened when it comes to understanding teamwork.
- You have a great deal to learn when it comes to working with your coworkers.
- You need to be more mindful of your team mentality during business hours.
- Everyone around here tries to get along with others; I would encourage you to do the same.
- Independent behavior won't get you far here.
- We have no room on our team for rogues or isolationists.
- There's four corners in the sandbox, but you're not even *in* the box.
- You're brilliant, but your inability to cooperate is going to break you, here.
- Your separatism and antisocial behavior need to stop—now.
- The next time I have to remind you to play well with others will be your last.
- Either you start working well with others or you're through, okay?
- Play nice or get the hell out.

Punitive

When an Employee Wastes Time/Procrastinates

Encouraging

- Just think how good it will feel to get all this off your plate!
- You'll be amazed at how much you can accomplish by sticking to a schedule.
- We've all had to learn self-discipline and the art of prioritizing.
- Would it help if we put our heads together and worked out a schedule for you?
- I know it's difficult; just tough it out until you're done with each project.
- Why put off until tomorrow what you can do today?
- You're a great employee. Please just try to stay on task.
- Everyone suffers when someone can't stay on target.
- You're not just wasting your time here, unfortunately.
- Do we need to look at revising your duties or responsibilities?
- Waste not, want not—especially when it comes to time management.
- Failure to plan only means that you can plan on failing.
- There are three things you can never get back: a word after it's spoken, a rock after it's thrown, and time after it's wasted.
- Wasting time in the workplace doesn't go over well here.
- It's exasperating being made to wait for someone to get her act together.

Punitive

- I expect everyone here to manage their time, and you are no different.
- Procrastinators like you sap the lifeblood from this company.
- Idle hands do the devil's work.
- It's really a shame how you fritter away all your time and talent.
- If wasting time were an Olympic sport, you'd win the gold medal.
- How is it that you can even function here?

When an Employee's Work Is Sub-Par

Concerned

- There seems to be a disconnect between you and your work lately. What's up?
- You seem to be having trouble keeping up. Is there anything I can do to help?
- Your work here has been suffering; talk to me about what's going on.
- What can we do to help you bring everything back up to par?
- I know how hard it is to keep pace sometimes, but you really need to try harder.
- Is there any way you can check your own work before submitting it?
- I know you can do better than this.
- Failure to meet expectations here needs to be the exception, not the rule.
- The quality of your work here needs to be improved, and soon.

Punitive

- Do you feel comfortable handing in the quality of work that you do?
- If you looked objectively at your performance, you'd realize just how abysmal is it.
- These chronic work deficiencies need to be addressed before harsher measures are taken.
- If you don't fix this soon, we may need to take harsher measures.
- A company of this size can't carry dead weights like you.
- It's not my responsibility to educate you about this stuff. I think you'd be happier elsewhere.
- I believe you've taken "sub-par" to a whole new level.

When an Employee Has an Attitude Problem

Concerned

- You seem really unhappy. Is there anything I can do to help?
- We all have bad days, but it's not fair to take it out on others.
- I understand you're feeling out of sorts, but you need to handle your emotions more effectively.
- I know it's hard to see yourself, which is why I am bringing this to your attention.
- It's everyone's job to maintain a pleasant and professional work environment.
- You can only control yourself and your reactions to others/situations.
- You can make a choice to be pleasant, as we all try to do.

- The way you're behaving makes me think your heart has left the station.
- Your bad attitude has become really bad for morale.
- You're bringing everyone down with your negative attitude; it needs to stop.
- No one wants to work with you, you're so grumpy.
- You have so much to offer, but the bad moods have got to go!
- I wish your emotional intelligence and people skills matched your talent.
- Copping an attitude here will help no one, especially you.
- What's with the attitude? Are you compensating for something?
- I think you need to take a few days off to think about how you've affected morale here.
- Did someone forget to take their "happy pill" this morning?
- I can't believe you got this far with such a negative attitude.
- Stop being such a prima donna and get back to work.
- You need an attitude adjustment. Take care of it, or we're through.
- Your attitude has become disruptive and toxic. We are going to need to let you go.

Punitive

When an Employee Is Bullying or Threatening Others

- Can't we all just get along? [*joking*]
- There must be a reason why you're acting this way–what's going on?
- Gosh, you seem really upset/angry. What seems to be the problem?
- When you hurt one person, you hurt everyone.
- I don't think you're making the wisest choice by acting out in this manner.
- I know you're not happy, but that's no excuse for this kind of behavior.
- Nobody here has the right to treat another member of my team unfairly or cruelly.
- Everyone here has an obligation to act in a professional manner.
- I don't think your behavior is helping anyone, least of all you.
- There is a time and a place for everything, *except* making threats to coworkers.
- You're spreading dissention with your bullying tactics, and I don't like it.
- You need a reality check if you think you can get away with that.
- We do not tolerate this kind of bullying behavior here–ever.
- It must be hard to get any work done when you're constantly having to watch your own back.
- Bullies are just cowards in disguise, you know.
- Being a bully will only hurt you in the long run.
- If you really feel the need to push someone around, just try pushing me.

Punitive

- You seem to lack the self-control required to work in a professional organization.
- This is a bully-free workplace. Deal with it.
- You need to change your behavior now or get out.
- It's time you picked on someone your own size; bring it on!

When an Employee Is Behaving Inappropriately

Concerned

- I'm sure you don't mean any harm, but you really need to rein it in.
- I'm a little confused as to why you would be acting this way.
- I'm a bit concerned about your behavior lately. What's going on?
- I don't want to see you go down the wrong road; I hope you can turn this around.
- There is a point beyond which it may be impossible to repair your reputation; think about that.
- I have been receiving a lot of complaints about your behavior. Care to explain?
- I think you may need to get help, your behavior is so outrageous.
- Why do you feel the need to constantly test the boundaries of what is socially acceptable?
- Your recent behavior has been attracting a lot of negative attention; is that what you want?
- I was once immature enough to pull those kinds of stunts, but that was a long time ago.
- People like you either straighten out or get left by the wayside.

Blunt

- The more you act out, the less your coworkers will think of you.
- This sort of immaturity and inappropriateness won't be tolerated here.
- Behaving like this is holding you back. Don't you want to succeed?
- You're out of control and you need to stop it now.
- No one wants to work with a jerk/weirdo, so stop acting like one.
- This isn't a circus and I'm not the ringmaster, so don't act like a clown.
- There is a time and a place for everything, except this kind of behavior.
- A word of advice: Straighten up and fly right, or go home.
- You're so far over the line, you don't even know where it is anymore.

When an Employee Always Plays the Victim

Encouraging

- I feel badly that you're upset, but let's try to stay positive.
- Rather than assign blame, let's figure out how to make things better.
- Life is 10 percent what happens to you, and 90 percent how you respond.
- A big part of success involves owning up to your mistakes and learning from them.
- Nobody wants to work with someone who constantly shifts blame onto others.
- Why not focus on cleaning up *your* side of the street?

Dismissive

- Stop worrying so much about other people and start focusing on your work.
- It's difficult to respect people who always try to garner pity.
- A victim mentality will never get you very far in life.
- If you do your work you won't have to worry about what others are doing.
- When you *really* need help, no one will believe you.
- You've played the victim for so long I actually believe you think it's true.
- I was on your side until I saw how you were milking this for all it was worth.
- I've seen you play the victim so often that I no longer know *what* to believe.
- Right, everyone's at fault except you. [*sarcasm*]
- Nobody wants to hang out or work with a martyr.
- Oh, buck up!
- Quit your bitching!

When an Employee Lacks Basic Hygiene

Subtle

- Ah, those glory days of going a week without showering in college are over. [*joking*]
- When you look and smell good, you feel good, too; wouldn't you agree?
- I read this great article on the best new men's/women's grooming products. Care to read it?
- I just love that clean, fresh, post-shower feeling, don't you?

- What was that old saying—cleanliness is next to godliness?
- I got a free trial size of this awesome new shower gel if you're interested.
- I think you'll be more comfortable if you bumped up the personal grooming a notch.
- Part of having a professional demeanor includes being well-groomed and immaculate.
- Please attend to your grooming and I promise I won't mention this ever again.
- I would encourage you to reread the company dress code policy again.
- The company expects a sharper and more immaculate image from its associates.
- Just a reminder that I expect *all* team members to freshen up before showing up to work.
- I think it would be best if you went home and freshened up.
- I can't have my employees meeting clients looking unkempt and bedraggled.
- Do you even check the mirror before you leave in the morning?
- Look—you stink, okay? Please take the time to shower every morning.

Blunt

Dealing With Sycophants

Accepting

- Ah, flattery will get you nowhere! [*joking*]
- Look, I really appreciate all the stroking, but it's not necessary, okay?
- Everyone loves compliments, but you're overdoing it a bit, don't you think?
- I appreciate the kind words, but try and stay focused on your work.
- I'm a big fan of genuine, authentic people who can speak the truth.
- I always prefer to hear the truth, even if it hurts.
- There is something inauthentic about sycophants, wouldn't you agree?
- No one respects a toady or a yes-man, least of all me.
- Flattery can be a useful technique, but only up to a point.
- Slavish devotion is not what I am looking for in my employees.
- Resorting to flattery to get ahead is one step away from prostitution.
- My shadow is feeling jealous because you're occupying the same space.
- You're trying to pump me full of hot air, but it's not going to work.
- Flattering well takes nuance and skill—skills that you do not have, unfortunately.
- Brownnosers and sycophants never make it very far here, just so you know.
- The motives for your flattery are transparent and, frankly, fairly off-putting.

Rejecting

- Honestly, I feel a bit skeeved out by your obvious toadying.
- Do you want to be seen as a person of integrity? Then stop all the falsity.
- You put the "sick" in "sycophant."

Dealing With Gossips

Subtle

- I'd love to hear all about this, maybe some other time when we're not so busy.
- I love a good, juicy story as much as anyone else, but not during work hours.
- Yes, enquiring minds want to know—just not on my watch.
- I'm concerned about all the gossip that's been flying around here lately.
- Hmm, does he know that you're talking about him this way?
- Maybe we should let that person know what you really think of her.
- All the backstabbing and trash-talking is negatively affecting morale.
- Take a moment to think about how your words are affecting everyone here.
- There is no place for gossip around here.
- When you gossip, I know you don't take your work seriously.
- I will not allow gossip and other hurtful communications to flourish here.
- If you can't say something to someone's face, you shouldn't say it at all.

Blunt

- If you can't say anything nice, I'd recommend that you keep quiet.
- This is all TMI; please keep it to yourself next time.
- Did you know that you are seen as a old biddy, constantly up in everyone's business?
- You won't be here much longer if you can't keep your hurtful stories to yourself.
- Did you know that there are legal ramifications for slander?
- Cut it out or I'll have to cut you loose.
- Knock off the malicious gossip or I'll have you fired.

Dealing With Complainers

Encouraging

- I know you can be a more constructive force in the workplace.
- Every problem has a solution; therein lies the real challenge.
- I understand the need to vent, as long as it doesn't impinge on your work.
- I know it's tough, but we all need to think on the bright side.
- We all have problems; what matters is how we deal with them.
- If you come to me with a complaint, I want to hear three possible solutions.
- Complaints are an opportunity to change for the better, but only if they are constructive.
- There's a saying: "When you keep stirring the crap, it keeps smelling."

Rejecting

- Complaining for its own sake, such as what you do, is an exercise in futility.
- No one wants to be around a Debbie Downer or a Ned Negativist.
- It's natural to want to complain, but we need to keep focused on why we're here.
- If you have a problem, I suggest you take it up with HR.
- How can one person have this many problems in life?
- You never seem happy here; maybe this job just isn't a good fit for you.
- You need to check your negative attitude at the door.
- Whining and complaining are counterproductive and will only get you fired.
- You should start volunteering at a soup kitchen; that will put your "problems" in perspective.
- There's really nothing I can do to help you. Maybe you should get some counseling.

Dealing With Loose Cannons

Respectful

- I love that you always speak your mind, but sometimes it's a bit unnerving.
- Being part of a group means that we subjugate our own desires and values somewhat.
- We all need to toe the company line, and you are no different.
- I'm not asking you not to be yourself, only to go with the flow.

Rude

- Freedom of speech is guaranteed under the Constitution, but this isn't a democracy.
- You seem to think you're exempt from our policies and procedures. Why is that?
- It would be better if you made more of an effort to fit in here.
- Is adjusting to the company culture really that difficult?
- If you focus only on your own viewpoint, you'll miss out on the insights of others.
- Always taking the opposing viewpoint doesn't make you right.
- Do you really think that, or do you just enjoy playing devil's advocate?
- Generally speaking, differences aren't tolerated very well here.
- People with a sense of entitlement rarely make it here.
- If you want to be a trailblazer, perhaps you would be better suited to entrepreneurial work.
- I never hesitate to fire people who refuse to bend to the rules.

Part 5

Motivation

When someone else blows your horn,
the sound is twice as loud.
—Unknown

Do you have trouble getting out of bed some mornings? Every morning? Well, your direct reports probably do, too. Motivation can be an issue in any job, whether you're an air traffic controller (let's hope not!), a masseuse, or a construction worker. Work is called work for a reason; it's not play, and sometimes people need a nudge every now and then to keep them on track and contributing to the bottom line. Most managers do this using Freud's pleasure-pain principle: they apply pain (confrontations, negative reviews, docks in pay, Machiavellian mind tricks) to stop negative behavior or underperformance; and they beneficently bestow pleasure (raises, bonuses, time off, SWAG with company logos) to reward them and keep the good stuff coming. There's still disagreement on what approach works best, and most managers tend to use one tactic more than the other. No matter your style, keep in mind that you are dealing with people, not robots. Personally, I like the Golden Rule when it comes to motivation: *Don't use any tactic on your direct reports that you wouldn't want used on you.*

How to Set Expectations

Vague

- There is no real way to measure success here; just do the best you can.
- It's hard to set expectations when everyone is so different.
- Just do your job and I won't have any problem with you.
- You know what you need to do. Do I need to spell it out for you?
- I expect everyone here to work hard and have fun. Any questions?
- I am not asking anything of you that I don't also expect from myself.
- I expect a lot from you, but I also expect a lot from myself.
- I set the bar reasonably high, so just do the best you can.
- I don't expect you to become a workaholic, but you need to do your share of heavy lifting.
- Be a strong self-starter and strong finisher; that's all I ask.
- If you kick ass here every day you'll have no problems.
- I'd to go over some goals for this quarter. Are you game?
- What are some concrete goals you think you should be shooting for?
- What would you think of getting X done by X date?
- My expectations for this year are pretty specific. Here they are....
- Here is exactly where I'd like you to be in X months. Is this doable?

Specific

How to Assign Tasks

Laissez-Faire

- I'm sure you'll find your own level here eventually.
- When you've figured out what you want to do, just let me know.
- Just figure it out yourselves; I'm not interested in micromanaging.
- I don't care who does what, as long as everything gets done.
- Do whatever you're most comfortable with and we'll figure out the rest.
- Everyone just needs to carry their own weight; the rest will work itself out.
- My goal is to get everything done; how that happens is up to you.
- I have my own ideas about how this can be accomplished, but I'd like to know how you'd do it.
- How would you like to approach/organize this task?
- How about we all draw names out of a hat to assign tasks?
- Please let me know what you'd like to do; I want everyone to be happy.
- We will break this assignment down into smaller tasks and then each person will choose one.
- I'd like to talk about assigning individual tasks. Everyone should let me know their preferences.
- Here is a breakdown of assignments and who does what. Let me know if anything needs to be changed.
- Here is the schedule for who does what. Any questions?
- This is how this is going to play out; I'll be looking at the results carefully when you're done.

Directive

How to Delegate Tasks

Nondirective

- You like this kind of stuff, right? Would you like to give it a try?
- This is a task that is uniquely suited to you. Why don't you give it a try?
- I think this would be right up your alley. What do you think?
- How would you feel about taking a crack at this?
- I know you're busy; could take this on right now?
- I think you'd be the best person to handle this particular job.
- While I'd like to think I can handle everything, I need you to take up some of the slack.
- I'd like you to step up and assume more responsibility in this particular area.
- I'm going to ask each of you to select a part of the project to make your own.
- I will delegate some tasks, but feel free to let me know if something doesn't suit you.
- Many leaders delegate because they lack confidence; I delegate because I trust you implicitly.
- I'd like you to handle this. Are you okay with that?
- I'm going to take each of you aside and explain your assignment.
- Everyone has a specific task to accomplish; if one fails, we all fail.
- It is critical that everyone here owns his assignment. It's all about personal responsibility.
- This isn't a democracy; either you choose or I'll choose for you.
- It ultimately comes down to this: I delegate, you do it, we all win.

Directive

- It's your turn. Show me what you can do!
- If I don't delegate I may as well relegate myself to the unemployment line.
- Your assignments are fixed and nonnegotiable. If you have any issues, take them up with HR.

How to Reward Excellence

Parsimonious

- I'd reward you, but I don't want to make the others jealous.
- For the conscientious worker, excellence is reward enough.
- We consider working here the highest reward of all.
- At the end of the day, an honest eight hours' pay is all the reward most people want.
- You're doing great—but don't take your foot off the gas yet.
- We're very proud of your dedication and hard work. Keep it up.
- As always, nice work.
- I knew I could count on you.
- I love that you love making me look good! [*joking*]
- I literally don't know what I'd do without you.
- Have I told you lately just how valuable you are to this company?
- We are all indebted to you and your outstanding work ethic.
- Our success is a direct result of the outstanding work you do here. Thank you!

Lavish

- I like to reward people like you who have gone the extra mile for the company.
- Keep up the good work and I'm sure you'll be compensated for it down the line.
- Your hard work and commitment will be rewarded at some point, I promise you.
- If you keep this up I think a bonus may be in the works.
- Given everything you've done, I'd like to reward you with a few paid days off.
- Because of your work in X project, you will be receiving a bonus of X amount.
- I am giving you a raise and the corner office. Congratulations!
- What would you like best: a vacation, a bonus, or a raise? Or would you like all three?

How to Provide Incentives

Begrudging

- The incentive I love to give most is continued employment.
- I'm not a big fan of rewarding one's reasonable service, but we can give it a try if you want.
- Most people don't need incentives to do a good job, but I guess we can try it out.
- Sometimes the cost of an incentive program negates the gain, but I'm willing to roll the dice.
- I love to have a little something to look forward to when my job is done.
- I'm thinking we need a little more carrot here, and a little less stick.

Lavish

- Since you need some motivation, here are the incentives for this project.
- Incentives usually don't help a chronic underperformer, but in your case maybe they will.
- Everyone needs something attainable to shoot for, so here is what I can do for you.
- Most of us need a little boost every now and then.
- I think these new incentives will help you keep your eyes on the prize.
- Incentives work much better than punishment, don't you agree?
- I believe this new incentive program will help everyone realize their goals.
- The carrot always works better than the stick, so who would like a carrot?
- What sorts of incentive would motivate you the most?
- I'd like to tailor these incentives to each person individually; that way, they'll be much more effective.

How to Build/Inspire Confidence

- As long as you do it tactfully, it's okay to blow your own horn once in a while.
- This world is a tough place for wallflowers. Don't let that be you.
- I bet your spouse/family/friends/coworkers are pretty proud of you.
- It's okay to toot your own horn from time to time, you know.
- You have every reason to be confident and self-assured.
- I wonder why you are so modest about your accomplishments.
- Confidence is something that is learned. Don't worry, you'll get there.
- Building one's confidence takes time. Just hang in there.
- If you act "as if," the confidence will be sure to follow.
- You could do so much if you just believed in yourself a little more.
- People would respond to you differently if you just carried yourself with more pride.
- The false modesty doesn't befit you at all.
- I'd like to see you acting a little more self-assured; after all, you've got "it" in spades.
- Your stellar skills/experience should make you much more confident than you are.
- Feelings follow actions; if you pretend you are confident, soon you will be.
- If I can develop confidence, *anyone* can.

Effusive

- I know you have that confidence in you somewhere.
- As a confident and self-assured person, you will go far in life; I just know it.
- If you throw a little confidence into the mix you'll be unstoppable.
- Once that penny drops, I know you'll be able to take on the world.
- Don't hide your light under a bushel; let it shine.
- There is no shame in showing off a little bit. Go for it!
- Don't be so modest.
- If you don't crow a little, I'll do it for you.
- You deserve all the accolades you can get.

How to Boost Your Team's Confidence

Subtle

- I'd like to see you guys projecting a bit more confidence.
- If you lack self-assurance, the world will eat you for breakfast.
- Without confidence, you've got everything to lose and nothing to gain.
- If you guys act "as if," the confidence will be sure to follow.
- There is no "confidence pill"; it's something that comes from within.
- You shouldn't doubt yourselves, because I certainly don't.
- I hired each of you because I know you can get the job done.

Directive

- There's no reason why you shouldn't be confident of your abilities as a team.
- You guys are far too modest. You should revel in your achievements.
- I know you guys can do anything you set your minds and hearts to.
- Together, you have the kind of power that can move mountains.
- There is nothing like a confident team that knows it can surmount any challenge.
- You all should feel confident that you can take on the world.
- How about showing me a little swagger?
- If you were honest with yourselves, you'd know just how great you are.
- Don't feel shy about your accomplishments; let them shine!
- Stop being so modest and be a little arrogant once in a while!

How to Praise an Employee

Restrained

- My thoughts are irrelevant; it's what you think of yourself that counts.
- Well, you've never let me down before.
- I've never had a complaint before, have I?
- I don't typically praise people, but in your case I'll have to make an exception.
- You do creditable work here.
- Yes, you did well. Now get back to work.
- In general you've done very good work.

- Your performance here is always decent.
- I'm proud of all you're done here.
- Please accept this gift card as a token of our gratitude.
- I don't know of a better employee, here or anywhere else.
- When I picture excellence, you immediately come to mind.
- You've outdone yourself once again.
- Your work ethic and integrity are to be commended.
- You have single-handedly raised the bar in this department. Well done!
- I'd like to recognize your work on this project by giving you a bonus.
- There is no way to reward you adequately, except perhaps by giving you the corner office and a raise.
- I'd like to formally recognize your achievements. What would be the most meaningful reward to you?
- What would be the best reward for all your hard work? I want it to speak directly to your achievements.
- You should be nominated for employee of the *year*.
- I do believe that I should be working for *you*.

Effusive

How to Praise Your Team

- You know how well you did. You don't need me to give you that information.
- If I'm not happy with your work, you'll know.
- You all always do a decent job.
- I have no complaints about your work here overall.
- You guys haven't let me down yet.
- In general I'm pleased with what you've accomplished here.
- Keep up the good work, everyone.
- This team is clearly a cut above the rest.
- Right now this team is raising the bar for all the other teams in the company.
- You guys are great—but don't start resting on your laurels now!
- I need to think of a way to reward performance for entire groups of employees....
- This company regularly recognizes team excellence, and now it's your turn.
- This team has outdone itself this month/quarter/year.
- No single team has ever done as much; you are all to be commended.
- I have never witnessed such excellence in a team. This is absolutely unprecedented.
- At this company we're used to excellence, but you've redefined the standards altogether.
- I am going to recommend this team for a special distinction/reward.

Effusive

- Please accept this reward on behalf of everyone on your team, as a token of the company's appreciation.
- I believe that this entitles every one of you to a paid day off/extra vacation days/a parking spot/etc.
- Because of your direct contributions, all of you will receive bonuses and raises.
- Because of your investment in this company, you will all be given stocks and profit-sharing.
- I want every one of you to feel appreciated and rewarded in a way that is meaningful to you.

How to Boost Team/Department Morale

Laid Back

- The beatings will continue until morale improves! [*joking*]
- I can't wave a magic wand and make it happen; it has to come from you.
- Look, these ebbs and flows are a part of life. Just roll with the punches.
- I know things looks bleak now, but I'm hoping they will get better.
- Don't worry, every group hits a bump in the road at some point.
- You guys will be okay once you get yourselves back on track.
- I've been through this, too, so know that you're not alone.
- We're all going to have to reach deep inside to find a new level of commitment.

Invested

- We need to figure out how to get our *joie de vivre* back. Any ideas?
- We are floundering and I want to fix that. How can I best encourage you guys?
- I have a plan to help get us out of this morass, I promise.
- Let's work together to figure out a way to rediscover our joy in our work.
- You have all the raw materials; all that's missing is that "holy fire."
- Getting our mojo back is a process, but together we can make it happen.
- I'm soliciting ideas for ways we can boost morale here.
- I have some concrete ideas for how we can make this a better place to work.
- I won't quit until we make this the best damn place to work in the world.

How to Nudge Underperformers

Encouraging

- How can I best help you fulfill your potential here?
- If I'm coming down hard on you, it's because I know you're capable of so much more.
- I have complete faith that you will be able to turn this situation around for the better.
- I know you have it in you; otherwise, I wouldn't have hired you.
- It's going to take some work, but I know you'll succeed if you really try.

- You have all the raw materials; you just need to ask a bit more of yourself.
- I know you're having trouble, but I am certain you will figure it out.
- You're like a diamond in the rough: You just need a bit more polishing.
- I know you can ask more of yourself if you just try a bit harder.
- What can we do to encourage you to raise the bar on your performance?
- I can see that you're in a rut, but I would like to help you out of it.
- When you fall off the horse, it's important to get back up and keep going.
- I'm very concerned about the quality of your work here; how can we help you improve?
- Your lack of performance is concerning and really needs to be addressed ASAP.
- This is not a job where you get a do-over every other day. You need to step it up.
- You're the only one who can help yourself right now. It's all about personal responsibility.
- You're really skating on thin ice; I'd advise you to make some improvements in your work, pronto.
- I'm really not sure how to help you anymore. Do you have any suggestions?
- I'm not sure it's worth the investment of time and money it would take to get good work out of you.
- Consider yourself on notice at this point. Either you improve or you're out.

Harsh

How to Mentor a Promising Employee

Subtle

- I'm here if you need me.
- You know I'm always here if you ever want to talk about your career.
- I wish there was some way I could help you avoid common pitfalls on your way to the top.
- Not everyone likes to be worked with one-on-one. What are your thoughts?
- A seasoned mentor could make a huge difference in your career. Think about it.
- Mentorship is often just the thing we need to help us unlock our potential.
- Have you ever thought about our mentoring program? I think you would benefit greatly.
- The company has a program for mentorship. You can enroll in it if you want.
- I've learned a lot throughout my career that I think might be useful to you.
- I've taken an interest in your career and would like to offer what advice I can.
- I'm certainly no expert but I'd be happy to impart what advice I can.
- Some wise person once showed me the ropes here; I'd like to do the same for you.
- I'd really like to take you under my wing; I want to see you fly!
- If you have the desire to succeed, I have the skills, experience, and time to mentor you.
- If you really want to get ahead, I think you should take advantage of this opportunity.
- I think you would be foolish to turn down an opportunity like this.

Directive

When an Employee Lacks Pride in His Work

Subtle

- Everyone here should feel a sense of pride in her accomplishments.
- You should feel very good about the good work you do here.
- There is nothing better than that feeling of a job well done, don't you think?
- Even the smallest, most insignificant job is worth doing well, wouldn't you agree?
- When people lack pride in their work, their work suffers as a result. Something to think about.
- If you took more pride in your work, I think you'd be surprised at the results.
- It's important that we take pride in everything we do here, wouldn't you agree?
- Tell me a little bit about how you are feeling about your work.
- You don't seem very keen on what you are doing here; do you think it's time for a change?
- You might want to consider rethinking how you view your work here. There's just a lot at stake.
- Why *wouldn't* you feel proud of what you do here? You do a lot for this company!
- If you derive no satisfaction from your work, your work will never improve.
- The fact that you lack pride in what you do tells me that you're not really happy here.
- Your lack of pride in your work is going to cause you problems, now and down the line.
- Do you feel no delight when you take a look at what you've accomplish?

Harsh

- If you obtain no satisfaction in what you do, I think you should find another calling.
- An employee who just goes through the motions will never make it here.
- How can I take pride in your work when you don't do so yourself?
- I see no way to help your attitude if you refuse to help yourself.

When an Employee Has Low Self-Esteem

Encouraging

- I know you're a winner, but you have to believe that in your own heart.
- Look, I think you're terrific, and you should, too!
- I'm amazed that someone so capable could doubt himself so much!
- Why do you get so down on yourself? There's absolutely no reason to!
- You have so much to offer; why would you think otherwise?
- Don't you think you should feel a little more positive about yourself?
- Self-esteem is what you need, but no one can give it to you.
- We all get down on ourselves from time to time, but you can't let it consume you.
- Your lack of confidence is hampering your enormous potential.
- You're obviously down on yourself a lot, but I fail to understand why.
- If you don't like yourself, no one else will, either.

Abrupt/Rude

- Nobody wants to hang around with an Eeyore.
- What happened to you as a child that you hate yourself so much?
- People with low self-esteem are just a turnoff to me, personally.
- Have you ever considered therapy for your lack of self-esteem?
- You are your own worst enemy. You have *a lot* of work to do.
- You really need to get yourself together, or you'll never make it here.
- Oh, knock off the pity party!
- Don't be such a masochist.

How to Encourage Innovation

Polite

- I know you have something more exciting than that up your sleeves.
- Maybe you need take a step back and look at it from a new perspective.
- It's time for something different than the "same old, same old."
- You can't fail or look foolish; just give me 20 outrageous ideas by EOD.
- The idea of thinking outside the box is a cliché, but it's apt nonetheless.
- Coming up with something new is 10 percent inspiration and 90 percent perspiration.
- Whenever I find myself getting stale I do something wild. It always helps kick-start my creativity.

- Sometimes innovation is just a matter of looking at the same thing through a different lens.
- I think we really need to embrace the motto "Think different."
- I think we are ripe for one of those eureka moments. Are you game?
- If you are truly creative that means you no longer fear failure.
- There are no mistakes here—only creativity and innovation.
- This is where the rubber hits the road; show me the best you can do on this one.
- Show me why I pay all of you the big bucks for your big ideas.
- The time to pull the rabbit out of the hat is now, people!
- Okay, I want you guys to really wow me this time!
- When you fail to innovate, all you will innovate is failure.

Part 6

When It's Personal

Facing a problem presents a much less vulnerable part of you than running from it does.

—Unknown

This is probably where some of you will cringe. *Do I have to hear about my assistant's personal life? Why can't we leave that stuff where it belongs—at home?* If you are asking yourself questions like these, perhaps you haven't yet realized that the line between work and personal life is no longer as clear as it once was. For some, there *is* no line; their work is their life (just think of Milton in the movie *Office Space*). And of course there is always the human element: You are not managing robots; everyone has a personal life—even you!

Have you ever had a personal problem that has spilled over into your work and affected it adversely? If so, how did it feel? What was your manager's reaction? Even you are very good at compartmentalizing, if you've lived long enough, chances are you've had a life situation that has impinged on your work. Divorce, death, marriage, illness, taxes—these are all a part of life. If you find yourself uncomfortable with empathy and commiseration, you can still address these things without sounding all treacle-y. Of course, if saccharine is more your style, have at it!

When an Employee Has a Death in The Family

Empathic

- This may be the hardest thing you can go through. Our prayers are with you.
- I lost a loved one, so I can relate to what you're going through.
- I feel terrible for you; please take as much time as you need—on us.
- Here is my home number; please call me if you need anything.
- How can we best support you during this difficult time?
- We understand and will do everything we can to get you through this.
- You can count on us to be there for you during this time.
- Let me know if you need anything; you know I'm here for you.
- People on the team have volunteered to help you with meals, laundry, etc.
- Nobody expects you to bounce right back into the thick of things.
- We offer support during times of bereavement; make sure you take advantage of that.
- Our employee assistance program is the best resource I can think of.
- You won't be terribly effective for a while, but you'll get through it with time.
- As they say, time heals all wounds.
- This, too, shall pass.
- She wasn't well, so this wasn't altogether sudden, right?
- We provide for a week off for bereavement. I hope that's enough time.

Distancing

- I hope you're able to come back soon; we really need you here.
- Since you're almost out of personal days, you'll need to use your vacation time.
- Will you be able to deal with this while keeping up with your work?
- So what are you going to do about your workload?
- I know you've had a death in the family, but the show must go on.
- I certainly understand that you're hurting, but I have a business to run and mouths to feed.

When an Employee Is Ill

Empathic

- I'm so sorry you're not feeling well. Please get better soon.
- We're not saving lives here. Please take all the time you need to get better.
- Oh no, I hope it's nothing serious!
- Sorry to hear that; if there's anything you need, please let me know.
- There's nothing worse than being sick. Take some time off and get well.
- Please don't come in; we don't want to catch it, too!
- It's better to rest up now than push yourself and get sicker later.
- Please take advantage of your sick leave and get some rest.

Distancing

- Get well soon; we need you here!
- It's not that I don't believe you, but we'll need a doctor's note for our records.
- Everyone gets sick from time to time, but we all need to push through as best we can.
- So there's no way you can make it in?
- Would it be possible for you to work from home?
- Shall I forward all your files to your home e-mail address?
- Can't you take some meds and just tough it out?
- I was able to work through my recent illness. What's your excuse?
- When someone is sick this often, their commitment is naturally called into question.

When an Employee Is Going Through a Divorce

Empathic

- No one should have to go through this. Take whatever time you need.
- You must be grieving terribly; how can we best support you during this time?
- I am so sorry for your loss. Is there anything I can do?
- My own divorce was awful, so I can relate to what you're going through.
- I have heard that divorce is like a death; please take some time to recover and practice self-care.
- We will do everything in our power to help get you through this.
- We all go through rough patches in life: that's why we all support each other here.

- You can count on me to take up the slack while you're gone.
- I can't imagine what you're going through, but I'm here if you need anything.
- I think you need to take a little personal time to help you get back on track.
- Others have gotten through this just fine, and you will, too.
- Things will be tough for a while, but you'll get through it; don't worry.
- We have an employee assistance program to help you through this.
- This probably makes you wish you'd never gotten married in the first place, doesn't it?
- Sometimes you just have to be willing to let go and move on.
- You're better off without him.
- I never liked her anyway.
- Are you sure you're handling this the right way?
- Hopefully you will be able to move on and concentrate on work again soon.
- If I were you I'd reach a quick settlement so you can get on with your life.
- Is this going to drag out for a long time?
- This is just a fact of life today. I really hope your work won't suffer.
- I am sorry you're hurting, but I have a business to run.
- We all have personal problems, but we can't let them affect our productivity.

Distancing

When an Employee Is Stressed Out

Empathic

- You seem stressed. Is there anything I can do?
- I know things are stressful right now; how can I best help you?
- I can see you're stressed. Have I loaded you up with too much work?
- I've never seen you so on edge. Talk to me about what's going on.
- Do you need help with anything? You seem upset.
- You seem to be under fire all the time. What gives?
- Stress is the number-one killer; I don't want my employees dropping like flies.
- Can we move some work off your plate? Or perhaps a vacation is in order?
- Is there something wrong that we can help you with?
- I know it's tough to put your emotions aside, but you need to try.
- Up until now, you've been my most steady worker. What's going on?
- We all feel stress; it's how you deal with it that counts.
- Be honest: Are you just unable to shoulder the workload here?
- There isn't a job in the world that come without stress. You're just not handling it well.
- It seems like your coping skills could use some brushing up.
- There's no avoiding stress; what matters is whether we can cut the mustard.

Harsh

- You really need to be more zen about everything.
- If you can't find your level here, maybe it's just not working out.
- Huh, I really thought you could handle the stress here.
- When I was your age there wasn't anything I couldn't handle.
- I can't have employees coming apart at the seams. Get yourself under control.
- We're all under pressure. You need to buck up.
- If you can't stand the heat, get out of the kitchen.
- Take a chill pill. You're making the rest of us anxious.

When an Employee Is Burned Out

Concerned

- You work harder than anyone I know. Take some time off and relax.
- You're a bit frayed lately. I think you should take a day off to unwind.
- You've got Stage One burnout. Let's not let this go any further.
- I know you're at the end of your rope. What can I do to help?
- You've been working overtime for too long; it's time for a respite.
- I see some symptoms of burnout here; I sure hope I'm wrong.
- We can't afford to let you burn out; how can we help?

- Everyone hits the wall every now and then. Would a lateral move help?
- We need to nip this in the bud before you do some real damage to yourself.
- This is a classic case of overwork. Do you think some time off would help?
- I don't know what we'd do if you flamed out for good.
- Is this really burnout, or is there something else going on?
- I think you should avail yourself of our Employment Services program.
- I'm not sure if you're really burned out or just lazy.
- Is your manager making life difficult for you or something? [*joking*]
- Most people with "burnout" just don't know how to manage their time.
- You job isn't harder than anyone else's here, so I'm not sure what I can do.
- I know several other people who have much better reasons to be frazzled.
- If you can't stand the heat, maybe it's time to get out of the kitchen.
- I'm not really familiar with burnout because most people who can't handle it here just leave.

Distancing

When an Employee Has Financial Difficulties

Compassionate

- The company would like to help you out until you get back on your feet.
- In this economy so many people are suffering. Is there anything we can do to help?
- We've all gone through financial ups and downs, so don't feel like you're alone.
- I'm a wiz at financial planning. If you're open, let's meet and see if we can create a plan.
- I'm not sure what I can do to help, but that doesn't mean that I don't care.
- I have an excellent book on finances and budgeting. If you like, I can loan it to you.
- Life is tough for all of us these days; we just have to make the best of what we have.
- Many people have gone through this; I'm sure you'll be fine.
- People in the Third World—now *they* have problems.
- I don't like to discuss financial matters with my employees unless it's affecting productivity.
- Your problems are a bit outside of my range of expertise, I'm afraid.
- You might want to look into a program to help you manage your finances.
- I've really got a lot on my plate right now. Are you sure this can't wait?
- Weren't you having the same issues a year ago?
- Have you looked into food stamps or the local soup kitchen?
- I know you're going through some lean times, but it's not like it's an emergency.

Distancing

- Most people who have financial problems create them themselves.
- If you can't handle your finances, how can you realistically handle this job?
- I understand you're having issues, but I do have a business to run.

When an Employee Seems Blue or Down

Compassionate

- I hate to see you going through this. Is there anything I can do?
- My heart goes out to you; please don't feel that you have to suffer in silence.
- I can see that you're struggling; please talk to me; I'm here to help.
- You seem sad. Is there something I can do to help?
- My door is open if you ever feel you need to talk or vent.
- I'm sorry to see you so out of sorts; is there a specific way I can help?
- I see depression just like any other illness, one requiring treatment and compassion.
- You seem really down and we're all starting to worry about you.
- Sometimes the best thing to do is just vent about your problems to a neutral third party.
- If you feel like this often, maybe you should look into getting treatment.

Distancing

- I sure hope I haven't contributed to your problems!
- This world is enough to make anyone feel blue; it's how we react to it that counts.
- Everyone has a bad day now and then, but it seems like this has gone on for a long time.
- Your productivity has really been slipping; is that what's causing your blue mood?
- We have a doctor/therapist on staff. I'd suggest you make an appointment.
- There are probably better people to talk to about this than me.
- I don't really like to get involved in the personal problems of my employees.
- I've felt down about things before, but I always try to carry on.
- I'm not sure that venting or dwelling on problems is the best plan of attack.
- Depression is a real illness, but I believe that many people are just malingering.
- We can't have you moping around here all day and affecting morale.

(Note: *Suicidal ideation, words, or actions should always been taken seriously.*)

When an Employee Is Dealing With Domestic Violence

Hands-Off

- I wish I was equipped to give you the help you need.
- We strongly encourage you to get whatever help you need.
- I feel terrible, but I don't want to pry into your private life if you don't want me to.
- I feel your pain but I am unsure how to help.
- Anger is one thing, but this person is going too far!
- We care about you too much to lose you.
- Do you think you should go to a shelter?
- The company has a handbook about domestic violence. Would you like a copy?
- If you stay with him much longer, you'll end up with Stockholm syndrome.
- You deserve to be treated with kindness and respect, you know.
- I believe you are one of those people who can break the chain of violence.
- In my opinion I think you should get out and get help.
- Please get out of this situation right away and seek help!
- You need to create a plan to get out; what can I do to help you?
- I want you to take as much time as you need to get yourself safe and away from this person.
- There are people here who would be happy to take you in. Here are their numbers.
- I want you to speak to this lawyer friend of mine so you know your rights.

Directive

- This person is bad news. You need to get out—*now*.
- I am not ordinarily so take-charge, but I can't stand to see you hurting like this.
- I'm taking you to the police station so you can press charges. Then, I'm taking you someplace safe.

(Note: If there is an imminent risk of danger to anyone, the only correct response is to contact the appropriate authorities and call 911.)

Part 7

Meetings and Presentations

*Meetings are indispensable when you
don't want to do anything.*
—John Kenneth Galbraith

Ah, meetings: the biggest time-waster of all time. And presentations? Don't even get me started. But they are a necessity in most companies, so you'll need to become comfortable with and good at managing both. As a manager, you'll need to lead (or least moderate/guide) meetings, and you'll need to be able to stand and deliver to your superiors when the time comes.

Maybe you know PowerPoint and maybe you don't, but your words are where the rubber hits the road. To make the most of these two necessary evils, make your words count!

How to Open a Meeting

- And how are we?
- How is everyone doing today?
- Okay, folks, let's get down to business, shall we?
- Somebody please bang the gavel and bring this fool's errand to order. [*joking*]
- Thanks so much for being here. I promise I will make this quick and painless. [*joking*]
- Very glad we could all meet today; thank you for coming!
- I'm pleased that we could all be here today. So what's first on the agenda?
- Thank you for being here today. We have only a few things to cover, so let's get started.
- I appreciate you all being here, considering how busy everyone is.
- Everyone please take your seats so we can get started.
- As master of ceremonies, I'm calling the meeting to order.
- I'd like to open this meeting and bring the proceedings to order.
- Allow me to welcome you all to this meeting. Let's begin with a few opening remarks.
- The time has come to call this meeting to order. Please direct your attention to the podium/front of the room.
- Without further ado, let us open our meeting notes and begin.

Formal

- Will everyone please be seated and address your attention to the front of the room.
- The meeting is now in session. Please read the minutes of the last meeting as Item One of the agenda.

How to Close a Meeting

Casual

- Last one to the bar is a rotten egg.
- Alrighty, let's get out of here!
- Well, that's enough for one day!
- That's all folks! [*joking*]
- Okay, I think we've covered everything. Any questions?
- Thanks for coming, all. See you next time!
- We're done with business for the day. Anyone up for lunch/drinks after work?
- Okay, until next time, then?
- Thank you all for being here. We'll meet again next week/month/quarter.
- This has been a great opportunity for discussion, but our time has just run out.
- I do believe we're done here. Let's convene again next week/month/quarter.
- I know we all have other matters to attend to, so let's adjourn until next time.
- Although this meeting has now come to a close, I hope you take away from it a spirit of camaraderie.

Formal

- Let us now call this meeting to a close and adjourn until next time.
- With the sound of the gavel the current session has officially come to a close.
- This meeting is hereby adjourned. Please mark the next session on your calendars.

How to Get the Attention of Your Audience

Humorous

- Are you all ready for some pearls of wisdom? [*joking*]
- I know you're out there; I can hear you breathing. [*joking*]
- If you've ever been where I am, looking out onto a sea of bored faces, you'll know the absolutely terrified I am right now. [*joking*]
- I admit I'm a bit nervous, so please go easy on me! [*joking*]
- Fasten your seat belts, folks; it's gonna be a bumpy night. [*joking*]
- Now, listen up; this is important!
- I know what you're thinking: *What the heck can she tell me that I don't already know?*
- I was once where you are, waiting for someone to saying something of importance.
- Whatever I say, please feel free to pick and choose what works for you and discard the rest.
- I know talk is cheap, but I am going to try to back up everything I say with actions.
- I am so very grateful for your time, and I will do my utmost not to waste it today.

Serious

- The next hour may be the most important one of your life.
- I am only a messenger; what you do with this critical information is up to you.
- Even you learn only one new thing here today, my work will not have been in vain.

How to Ask for Help

Subtle

- Gosh, I wish there was someone who could help me with this.
- Honestly, I feel like I am floundering.
- I don't think I can handle this on my own.
- Are you really busy right now? Oh, never mind.
- Isn't it great how we all pitch in and help one another around here?
- There's a time and a place for going it alone, and this isn't one of them.
- Only a fool refuses help when it's offered—or refuses to ask for help when it's needed.
- Sometimes I wish people here could just spot a need without my having to spell it out.
- I'd welcome any support or backup you could offer.
- It would be so great if you could get in on this project.
- I hate to ask you this, but would you be so kind as to give me a hand with this?
- You know I would help you if you needed it, so I'd hope you'd do the same for me.
- I'm just asking you to do what you can, that's all.
- Can someone help me, please?

More Direct

- Would you please give me a hand with this? I'd appreciate it.
- Please—I just can't do this alone.
- I need your help—like, *now.*
- When your manager asks for help, you deliver.

How to Give Bad News

Tactful

- I have something fairly important to tell you. Can we talk for a moment?
- Something's come up and we need to talk. Is this a good time?
- I will do my best to break this news to you gently.
- There's something I need to tell you, and I don't really know how.
- This is very hard for me, so please be patient with me as I try to get this out.
- Please don't kill the messenger, but I have some bad news to relate.
- I will try to make this as easy as I can on you.
- Why do I always have to be the person to say these things?
- You may have already heard this, but I have a bit of bad news, unfortunately.
- I'm going to try to make this as painless as possible. Here goes.
- There's just no easy way to say this, so I'll just say it.
- There is never a good time to give bad news, so I'll just get it over with.

- I simply can't sugarcoat this situation, so I won't.
- Let's just get this over with, okay?
- Nobody is ever ready to receive news like this, so just brace yourself.
- I'm not particularly good at delivering bad news, so let's get this over with.
- This may come as a shock, so please prepare yourself for what I'm about to say.
- I have some terrible news, so brace yourself.
- Let's just cut to the chase, shall we? It's bad.
- I have bad news. Take it like a man.

How to Recap Key Points

- One more time, with feeling. [*joking*]
- I don't know about you guys, but I need to review before moving on.
- Okay, let's go over this stuff again.
- Let's recap, okay?
- I'm sure your brains are in overload, so let's recap, okay?
- Anyone here care to sum things up for the rest of us?
- Let's go back over what we just covered so we're all on the same page.
- Let's take a moment to go over the main points of our discussion.
- There is no way we'll absorb all this without a complete recap.
- I think we need to go over our findings once more in a general way.

Formal

- I think we need to backtrack and go over the key points once more.
- It's important that we have a solid understanding of where we've been before moving on.
- Let's sum up our findings as bullet points, shall we?
- There is no time like the present to go over the major points of the meeting so far.
- We want to keep everything fresh in our minds, and a good recap will accomplish that.
- I would like to recap our findings so that we can have a better idea of where to go next.
- A summation of the major points is needed before we continue.
- It's important that we go over the salient points before continuing the meeting.

How to Propose a Solution or Solutions

Gentle

- This may sound crazy, but what if we considered this instead?
- I could be wrong, but this might be a possible solution.
- I'm not sure what else I can add, but have we thought about this?
- I am wondering if this might be of help.
- Do you think something like this might be a possible solution?
- Your solution is good, but have we explored all the options?
- Has anyone considered an alternative such as this?

Blunt

- I think we need to consider other options, such as...
- I believe something like this would be worth looking into.
- What would we have to lose to at least consider this as a solution?
- What if tried doing something different, such as this?
- I think there is a better way to handle this, if you're open to hearing it.
- I think we need to stop debating and go with a workable solution, such as this.
- Until we discover a reasonable or better alternative, we need to go with this.
- Sorry, but I'll need to exercise my veto power on this one.
- We're doing it this way and that's the end of it.
- All of your solutions are non-starters; we're doing this instead.

When You Need to Instill Calm

Gentle

- I think we all need to just breathe and relax for a moment.
- I know we are all upset; let's take a few minutes to compose ourselves.
- Please, everyone, let's take a moment to gather our thoughts.
- Everyone please calm down. It's impossible to hear anything in this melee.

Directive

- I'm upset, too, but this will be much easier if everyone just calms down.
- When people panic, bad decisions are made; everyone, please, just stay calm.
- We need to stay calm if we are going to handle this situation well.
- If we can't have peace, I'm afraid I'll have to clear the room.
- Everybody here needs to take a chill pill.
- Everyone, *please*—try to stay focused, okay?
- We're getting nowhere with all this commotion. Quiet down!
- Quit all the static out there and pipe down!
- I don't care how upset you all are; you need to shut up and listen!

How to Deal With Hecklers

Friendly

- I hear you; just give me a moment and then you can have the floor, okay?
- I am asking you politely to please allow me to finish my thought; will you do that?
- Please be seated; you'll get your turn to speak, I promise you.
- Please let me finish before you start interrupting me.
- If you will just wait a moment you'll have a chance to speak.
- You will be given an opportunity to speak, but only if you wait your turn.

- I know you have a valid point, but you still need to let others have their say.
- I want to work with you, but I can't when you're behaving like this.
- We may have to agree to disagree on that point.
- I'm not sure what, if anything, this person has to offer that could possibly be of value.
- You are exercising your right to free speech–I get that–but please give me a chance to finish.
- If you want to have your say, then allow everyone else to be heard, too.
- Your behavior is ungentlemanly/unladylike.
- Shouting and heckling never solved anything, you know.
- Would you care to enlighten the rest of us with your antics?
- I will tolerate disagreements and even dissention, but not rudeness.
- You are making it difficult for everyone here to take you seriously.
- Please be seated and wait your turn, or you'll have to be escorted from the premises.
- I refuse to give in to these tactics, which are meant only to unsettle me.
- Why don't you go back into the cabinet from whence you came?
- Shut up or I'll have you thrown out.

Confrontational

How to Admit You Were Wrong

Contrite

- I am ashamed of committing such an egregious error. It will never happen again.
- I was wrong, and I'll do anything to regain your trust in me.
- There is no excuse for what happened; please forgive me.
- I take full responsibility for what went wrong. I feel terrible about what happened.
- I absolutely dropped the ball here; please accept my apologies.
- This error is mine to correct and no one else's.
- I should have listened to you in the first place—my bad.
- Gee, I was seriously off base; lesson learned, I guess.
- I was definitely in the wrong about this one. Whoops.
- It was an honest mistake that could have happened to anyone.
- I feel pretty bad about what happened; just luck of the draw, I guess.
- To err is human; but to forgive is divine, apparently.
- I did the crime, so now I guess I have to do the time. [*joking*]
- My only error was in not acknowledging my mistake sooner.
- Yes, I was wrong—but isn't everyone from time to time?
- I was just a victim of circumstance.
- Sure, I made a mistake. I admit it. How many have *you* made?

Less Remorseful

- Who are you to point a bony finger at me?
- You got me! Happy now?
- Yeah, yeah. I was wrong. Now can we get on with things?
- Yep, I'm the bad guy in this situation. [*sarcasm*]
- Mea culpa. [*sarcasm*]

When the Company/Industry Is Facing Tough Times

Casual

- There are no easy answers in times like these; we just need to keep our heads down and stay focused.
- The beatings will continue until morale improves. [*joking*]
- If adversity is what introduces a man to himself, I think we're going to get to know ourselves *real* well over the coming months. [*joking*]
- Times are tough all around, I'm not gonna lie. But I am right there with you.
- I know this sucks, but let's be glad that we're still in business.
- If you're going through hell, keep going.
- If we all stick together as a team, we'll be able to weather this storm just fine.
- This is just a dry spell, something we can weather if we all pull together.
- Can't say how long this will last, but with your help I know we will make it through.
- If ever there were a time to buckle down and think realistically, that time is now.

Formal

- We all need to tighten our belts and start thinking about what we can do to help.
- We must all be prepared to meet these challenges together.
- Don't give up. This is a burden that can be shared among all of us.
- These are the times that try men's souls.
- If we keep rowing through the storm, we'll make it through.
- To make it through these challenging times, it's essential that we keep our eyes on the prize.

How to Announce a Merger, Acquisition, or Company Closing

Tactful

- What I am about to tell you affects the entire company, so please listen carefully.
- I have something extremely important to tell all of you.
- I've got some big news that will affect everyone in this room, including me.
- Most of you have already heard the rumors, but let's talk about what's really going on.
- There is just no easy way to say what I am about to say, so let me just come out with it.
- I'll try to put this as delicately as I can.
- Before I lose my nerve completely let me just spit it out.
- It's unfair of me to draw this out any longer, so here it goes.

- If you had to tell someone bad news, how would *you* do it?
- I'm giving you this crummy news because it's the right thing to do.
- I need to spill the beans about something that you've probably figured out already.
- I'm telling you this on a need-to-know basis; most definitely, everyone here needs to know this, *now*.
- Here is why management has been walking around looking like doom and gloom lately.
- We are no longer the masters of our own fates, it seems.
- As of X date we will be officially acquired/closed for business/shut down. Meeting adjourned.
- Not to put too fine a point on it, but we're going under/being acquired and we're all out of a job.
- Another company has taken control of our business. It's every man for himself now.
- The less said the better: This company as we know it is kaput.

Blunt

Part 8
Sticky Situations

A smooth sea never made a skillful mariner.
—Unknown

Just when you think you've prepared for everything, something comes and hits you out of left field. Maybe it's an employee who makes a pass at you. Maybe it's your boss who chooses to criticize you to your face—in front of others. Maybe it's two employees who decide they need to work things out with their fists. This is the stuff of which management nightmares are made.

Other than your company handbook, there really isn't any official playbook on how to handle these kinds of situations. But hopefully, with the right talking points, you'll be able to open every conversation—or confrontation—with more confidence.

When an Employee Criticizes You to Your Face

Tactful

- I see all criticism as an opportunity to make things better.
- I'd be more than happy to discuss whatever issues you have with me in private.
- Let's talk about this and resolve whatever's bothering you.
- You're obviously upset about something; what can I do to make this right?
- I can see why you might feel that way. Let's talk about this in private.
- I hear you and understand; what can we do to fix this?
- I'm glad we got that out in the open; now let me address your complaints.
- While I appreciate your honesty, I must say that what you just said stings a bit.
- I appreciate the feedback, although it's not what I would hope to hear from one of my employees.
- Well, I'm not sure that I would agree with you there.
- You are entitled to think whatever you want, but at the end of the day I'm still your boss.
- I'm sorry that you feel that way.
- Do you really think that was a constructive thing to say?
- Your opinion is duly noted for the record.
- You should be a bit more careful in how you speak to your higher-ups.
- We all need to vent from time to time, but you need to rein in the personal rancor.
- While this is a democracy, we all need to express ourselves appropriately and constructively.

Blunt

- You know, I've really grown fond of our little chats. [*sarcastic*]
- Please, tell me how you *really* feel. [*sarcastic*]
- Are you finished?
- Well, I guess it takes one to know one.
- Thank you for giving me yet one more reason to let you go.

When Two Employees Get Into a Physical Altercation

Conciliatory

- Wait—let me go grab a chair so I can watch the fur fly.
- Go ahead and knock yourselves out—just not on these premises.
- If you must go to these lengths, please take it outside, okay?
- Look, I'm all for working things out physically— just not here!
- Have you guys thought about starting your own personal fight club? [*joking*]
- Whoa, let's keep things professional, people!
- Either you two kiss and make up, or I'll *make* you fight.
- I don't think that getting physical does anyone any good.
- Please confine your conflicts to the boxing ring, not the boardroom.
- Ordinarily I enjoy a good fight, but not when it involves two of my best employees.
- Why can't you guys just agree to disagree and call it a day?
- This is neither the time nor the place for a smackdown.

- Why does everything have to end in fisticuffs around here?
- You guys need to figure out a way to make things right without resorting to violence.
- I'm sending you two home for a time-out. I suggest you make the best of it.
- I can't believe you lack the basic self-control to work things out professionally.
- I'm afraid you're both going to have to face the consequences of your behavior.
- If I find you guys smacking each other around again, I'm afraid I'll have to report it.
- The company has a strong policy against violence during working hours. I suggest you reread it.
- You can cut it out or I'll have to cut the both of you—from the payroll.
- If this nonsense continues you'll leave me no choice but to let both of you go.
- There is no excuse for this kind of behavior. Cut it out or you're gone.
- This company has a strict anti-violence policy. Pack up your desks and get out.
- Nobody resorts to violence here and gets away with it. You two are through.

Antagonistic

When an Employee Comes On to You

Tactful

- I thought you were more professional than that.
- I'll give you a chance to take back what you just said.
- While I appreciate the compliment, I don't think it was appropriate for work.
- Look, I'm flattered, but we need to keep things professional here.
- You're attractive, but I don't get involved with coworkers.
- Tempting, but I just couldn't respect myself in the morning. [*joking*]
- Sorry, I'm a one-man woman/one-woman man. [*joking*]
- I'm just going to go ahead and nip this in the bud before it goes any further, okay?
- If you think this over I think you'll realize just how foolishly you're acting.
- This is only going to get *you* in a lot of trouble.
- Are you sure you want to go around acting like that with your higher-ups?
- Your behavior is completely out of bounds, and I'm going to have to ask you to stop.
- There is no excuse for such unprofessional behavior. It needs to stop.
- If you don't stop I'll be forced to report your behavior to HR/the boss.
- Stop right now or I'll have to take action that you won't like.
- There is a company policy against fraternization. I suggest you familiarize yourself with it.
- Wow, you're a lot stupider than I thought.

Rude/Blunt

- What you're suggesting is the stupidest, most inappropriate thing I've ever heard.
- You're so far over the line, you don't even know where the line is anymore.
- No thanks, not interested.

When You Are Unable to Pay Your Employees

Tactful

- I don't want to sugarcoat this situation, but we're not where we want to be financially.
- I feel terrible about this, but please know that I am going without pay, too.
- We're in a bit of a sticky situation here, and I am asking for all of you to be patient.
- We've all been in a situation where money is a tight, right? This is no different.
- The company is good for your salaries, but you're just going to have to wait a bit.
- I would pay you out of my own pocket if I could, but I'm personally tapped out.
- Please wait to cash your checks until tomorrow/ next week/next month.
- We are obviously having cash flow problems, and I'm asking for patience while we sort it out.
- Unfortunately the company's problems just became everyone's problems.
- Please give us a chance to make this right.
- No amount of complaining will make this situation magically better.
- Please buckle down and get back to work. We'll figure this out, I promise.
- Well, there have been times you haven't put in a full day's work, either.

- If you were in my position, you'd understand how difficult it is to cover all the bases.
- I just can't pay you guys right now. Sorry.
- Maybe this is God's way of telling you to work harder.
- Stop complaining. The money will be paid out when it's ready.
- If you're that unhappy with the situation, you're free to leave.

Blunt

When Someone Tries to Pick a Fight With You

- I can see that you're upset. Let's take a break to calm down and gather our thoughts.
- I know you're seething, but I want to make things right with you.
- I know you're itching for a fight, but I just can't go there; I'm sorry.
- You talkin' to me? [*joking, á la Robert DiNiro in Taxi Driver*]
- Will fighting about this really help you in the long run?
- I think it would be better if we could reason this out like two adults.
- Are you really sure you want to go there with me?
- I'd fight you, but it's unfair to have a battle of wits with an unarmed person.
- If I weren't your boss I would be more than happy to show you my martial arts skills.

Conciliatory

Confrontational

- I suggest that you check yourself before you land yourself in a world of hurt.
- Company policy doesn't allow bosses to knock out their inferiors.
- I never get physical with my employees, no matter how much of an ass kicking they deserve.
- You have no idea how close I am to popping you right now.
- Okay, but you shouldn't bring a knife to a gunfight.
- Go ahead, hit me—but I promise you'll regret it.
- Take your best shot, because it's the only one you're going to get.
- Oh, grow up and knock it off!

When an Employee Threatens You or Others

Conciliatory

- I'm sure this is my fault. Can we sit down and talk about this?
- I can see you're upset, but we need to discuss this rationally.
- I know you didn't mean that; just take a breather and compose yourself.
- I understand you're upset, but I think you need to decompress a bit and calm down.
- I want to talk to you about this when you are calmer.
- I think you need to rethink what you just said and restate it.
- There such a thing as free speech, but you need to state things in a less threatening manner.

Confrontational

- Your words are making people feel uncomfortable and unsafe.
- Why would you say something like that? That's pretty harsh.
- Trust me, you don't want to go there.
- I will not allow this kind of talk from you or anyone else here.
- This is no place to start going off and making idle threats.
- Threatening people is completely against company policy.
- If you can't rein it in and act professionally, I'll have to ask you to leave.
- You've stepped so far over the line that you don't even know where the line is anymore.
- Now there's an idea: You threaten me, and I report you to the powers that be.
- We have a no-tolerance policy for that kind of talk; I'm going to have to report it.
- You need to leave—*now.*
- I am calling the authorities/security/the police.

(Note: *In the event of legitimate threats or real danger, you should always call 911.*)

When an Employee Throws a Tantrum

- Wow, I can see you're at your wit's end. Let's go outside and walk for a bit.
- It's understandable that you're upset; just go somewhere private where you can let off steam.
- Let's everyone just calm down and talk this through.
- Tantrums will never get you anywhere around here. Now what is it that you need?
- Whoa, I think someone needs to take a chill pill. [*joking*]
- We all go through times when we feel like we're gonna lose it, but this is going a bit far.
- I know you're upset, but this can't happen again, you understand that.
- If you can't keep your cool maybe you should step outside and calm yourself down.
- Your behavior is making others feel really uncomfortable.
- Don't you have any self-control?
- I thought you had moved past these outbursts, but evidently I was wrong.
- When you blow up like this, you're affecting the morale of the whole company.
- You're not a wild beast in a cage; you're a human being with a job to do.
- I think you may need anger management training.
- Clearly, you need professional help; don't come back until you've gotten yourself under control.
- How can you expect to work with people if you go around acting like that?

Confrontational

- No one is allowed to behave that way on my watch. Either it stops or you're out.
- If you do it again, I'll be forced to reassign/fire you.
- By all means, keep going. I'm going to enjoy watching you get yourself fired.

When an Employee Is Drunk or High on The Job

Concerned

- I'm saddened to see you in such a state. What can I do to help?
- What is going on with you? I am really concerned about your behavior.
- Everyone needs to release stress sometimes, but this is only hurting you.
- You're so much better than this, you know?
- You need to deal with your stress in a way that doesn't hurt you or put your job in jeopardy.
- This may seem like a solution, but it's only going to compound your problems.
- We have resources for employees who struggle with substances and addiction.
- We have a program here that might be able to help you.
- If you need drugs or booze that badly, you obviously need help.
- I have no idea what you're on, but you've put me in a really awkward position here.
- We have a policy against this kind of thing on the job. I suggest you read it.
- I simply can't allow you to be drunk/high on the job. It's unacceptable, dangerous, and illegal.

Punitive

- No one is allowed to drink or do drugs on company time. Why should you be any different?
- You're useless to me like this; go home, and don't come back until you detox.
- I am going to have to report this to HR/the boss.
- We have a no-tolerance policy for this sort of thing. You're fired.

Part 9
Dealing With Customers

Nowadays people know the price of everything and the value of nothing.
—Oscar Wilde

Customers: They are the lifeblood of your company, but they can also be the bane of your existence—and vice versa! There is no limit to the number of customer service horror stories: the company that literally refuses to hear customer complaints; the unsatisfied, unsatisfiable customer who inexplicably keeps on coming back, seemingly just to make everyone's life a living hell. Wouldn't it be great if there were some ready-made words and phrases you could offer to your reports to help them through these sorts of situations? Fortunately, there are!

Of course, if your company has a track record of abysmal customer service, a few pat phrases are not going to change that; that's a top-down issue. But each and every person can still make a positive difference in every interaction, and it can all start with you. Set a good example with your employees, and they will be sure to follow. After all, you are all each others' "customers," in a sense. Start from the inside out, and you'll be shocked at how quickly and easily you can turn things around.

When Dealing With an Irate Customer

- It will be my pleasure to fix this for you immediately.
- There is a lot of validity to what you say. Please allow me to make this right.
- You are the customer, and the customer is always right.
- Your dissatisfaction is unacceptable to me. What can I do to make this right?
- I totally understand; I promise I will do everything in my power to satisfy you.
- I can see you are upset; what can I do to turn things around?
- Please tell me what you want and I will make it happen, I promise.
- I totally understand why you would feel this way; is there anything I can do to help?
- You have every right to feel as you do. Lay it on me; I can take it.
- Your complaint is certainly valid, but you need to speak respectfully.
- Please speak respectfully to me and I will do my utmost to help you.
- I truly believe we can work something out, as long as you calm down and speak nicely.
- I understand you're irate, but please do not shout at me/speak to me that way.
- I want to help you, but you are making it difficult for me to focus on the problem.
- Let's figure out a way to turn this around, shall we?
- If you insist on being rude it makes it hard for me to focus on a solution.

Confrontational

- I think I'll be able to help you better if you calm down and speak respectfully to me.
- I am trying hard to help you, but you need to meet me halfway, here.
- There is no need to lose your temper. We're all trying to help you as best we can.
- People like you give all customers a bad name.
- I've dealt with customers like you before. Usually you just move on to torture someone else.
- I don't think this relationship is working out; perhaps you'd be happier elsewhere.
- I need to leave before I say something I will regret.
- I don't have to stick around and take this kind of treatment.
- No one talks to me that way—nobody.
- This is outrageous. You need to leave.
- I've never heard such a load of crap in all my life.
- I have nothing further to say to you; it's best if you left.
- We don't need customers like you around here.

When a Customer Is Demanding a Refund

Conciliatory

- I am so sorry you are unhappy. Please let me rectify the situation to your satisfaction.
- Of course, it would be my pleasure. Is there anything else I can help you with?
- It would be my pleasure to give you a refund. Please accept X as a token of our goodwill.
- Your satisfaction is our number-one priority. Allow me to help you.

- Your happiness is our first priority; we will do whatever we can to ensure that.
- I would be happy to give you a refund. Is there anything else I can do to make it up to you?
- I'm sorry we couldn't satisfy your needs. I'll have the full amount refunded immediately.
- I can see why you would want a refund, given your unhappiness with the product/service.
- We value you as a customer. Let me see what I can do for you.
- I'm sure that we can come to some agreement. Give me just a moment.
- I don't think the refund will be a problem, but I wish we had known about this sooner.
- I need to get my manager's approval before I do anything for you.
- Would you be willing to exchange the item for something different instead?
- It's our policy not to give refunds after X days, but in your case I'll make an exception.
- Without a receipt, I can only offer you store credit.
- Sorry—I can't do anything without a receipt.
- I wish I could help you with this; is there anything else you need?
- Would you offer a refund if *you* heard a story like that?
- I'd help you now but it's my lunch break. Can you come back in an hour?

How to Woo Back a Once-Loyal Customer

Casual

- You can't imagine how many changes we've made; I hope you'll give us another chance!
- We thought long and hard about why people like you left and made some real changes.
- We really miss your business and will do anything to get it back.
- I promise we will make it worth your while if you return.
- I feel terrible that we lost your business; what can we do to bring you back into the fold?
- I hate that we had a falling out; can we start fresh?
- Things here are *very* different now. Please let me prove it to you.
- Let's let bygones be bygones; I think you will be happy with us if you just give us a chance.
- I'm willing to give it another go if you are.
- Work with me again and I promise I will make it worth your while.
- I know you were once unhappy with us; what can I do to change your mind?
- Would you at least hear me out on what we can do to satisfy you, going forward?
- I'd love to have you back as a customer; what do I need to do to make that happen?
- We are ready and able to start over, if you are willing to give us a chance.
- We failed and learned a hard lesson. Please let us earn back your trust.
- Here are the measures we've taken to ensure that this will never happen again.

Formal

- We would like to win you back as a customer if you are amenable.
- Your unhappiness was simply unacceptable; here is what we can do for you, going forward.

When a Customer Wants to Speak to a Manager

Amenable

- I know exactly how you feel. I'll find my manager right away.
- My first goal is to find you a manager right away.
- Of course, let me get her for you right away.
- Absolutely—I will call my manager immediately.
- I agree that this situation calls for a manager. I'll call him over right away.
- I understand how you feel. Let me see what I can do.
- Tell me what you'd like and I will convey that to her asap.
- Sure, but I'd like to stay involved in the conversation if that's okay.
- Sure, I'll call the manager, but there is nothing he can do for you that I can't.
- There's no reason why I can't help you, though.
- There's no reason you *shouldn't* speak to a manager, but what is it you want, specifically?
- We have several managers on duty right now. I'll see if any of them are free.
- I'd really like to try to help you before calling other people into the mix.
- Okay, but I'm really not sure what you think you're going to get out of it.
- I'm unsure how she will be able to help you with this problem.

Rejecting

- You should probably take a number; everyone's a bit busy.
- No one is available right now; would you like to come back later?
- You'll just have to wait; your request is no more important than all the other requests.
- You'll need to come back some other time.
- I'm not sure that anyone here, management included, can help you with this problem.
- You're just going to have to deal with me—sorry.

When a Customer Is Getting Abusive

Empathetic

- I feel your pain and agree; how can I best help you today?
- I'm very sorry that you feel that way. What can I do to help?
- Let's sit down and discuss this rationally; I truly want to help you, okay?
- I want to understand where you're coming from. Can you explain it again?
- I think we'll have a better chance of helping you if everyone can keep their cool.
- I think we've officially hit bottom here; let's start over.
- I understand you are upset, but you need to calm down in order for me to help you.
- You have a point, but please speak respectfully to me.
- I will do my best to help you, even though it's against my better judgment.

- You are entitled to your opinion, but you need to change your tone of voice.
- I will be more than happy to help you if you calm down and speak respectfully.
- I want to help you, but you are making it difficult when you insult me like that.
- You really need to calm down. I can't talk to you when you're shouting at me.
- You've got to control yourself or we won't be able to help you.
- Your words are hurtful and uncalled for; please think before you say anything else.
- This approach will get you nowhere, fast.
- You're never going to get anywhere in life unless you lose the 'tude.
- It's amazing how you worked yourself up in such a short amount of time.
- After a tirade like that I'm predisposed to not listen to you at all.
- There is really no relationship here left to save, is there?
- You're free to be abusive if you want, but I'm also free to refuse you service.
- We don't need customers like you.
- If you can't calm yourself down, I will have to call security.

How to Find Out a Customer's Needs

Subtle

- Would you be okay with telling me a bit more about what's important to you?
- I have a feeling you have something specific in mind. Am I right?
- Can you give me an idea of the kinds of problems you are looking to address?
- If you told me a bit more about your needs, I'd be better able to assist you.
- I don't need to know *everything* about you—just enough to help me help you get what you want.
- I promise that whatever you tell me will remain strictly confidential.
- I don't have a Ouija board, but I think I have an idea of what you need.
- I think I'm a pretty good judge of people; let's see if I'm right.
- Without a little more information it'll be impossible for me to help you.
- Don't be coy; just tell me what you're looking for!
- So, tell me more about *you*: What are your likes? Dislikes? Interests? Pet peeves?
- Okay, there must be *some* specifics that are guiding your purchase. What are they?
- You're making it difficult for me to help you when you play your cards so close to your chest.
- More information equals better help.
- There's a limit to what I can do by myself. Help me out here!
- Just help me, help you!
- If you don't give me something to go on you're just wasting my time.

Pushy

How to Persuade the Reluctant Buyer

Subtle

- I'm going to help another customer while you think.
- Please take as much time as you need to think it over.
- You're thinking with your head right now; what does your *heart* say?
- It just feels like this was meant to be, don't you agree?
- I realize it's a major decision; why don't you take a few moments to think about it?
- If you're worried about buyer's remorse, you can always return it.
- I completely understand your reluctance, but I am backing this product with my very reputation.
- I feel that this is a great opportunity, and I think you'll feel that way, too.
- I think the pros far outweigh the cons in your case.
- All you need to do is sign on the line that is dotted. [*joking*]
- What are your objections? I think I can put every one of them to rest.
- There comes a time when you need to take the plunge and just make a decision.
- If you wait, there may not be another opportunity like it for a long time.
- I put a lot of effort into helping you/answering all your questions. What's it gonna be?
- I can tell that you want it; why not just go for it?

Overt

- C'mon, what do you say? You won't regret it, I promise!
- If you miss out, you'll kick yourself later!
- No one deserves it more than you. Just say yes and make me a happy guy!

Part 10
Managing Lower-Level Managers

Become the change you wish to see in the world.
—Gandhi

Most of this aspect of your job will be about setting an example with your behavior and your communication style. If you model respect, investment, kindness, tenacity, courage, and discipline, in both word and deed, there's a good chance that those who manage beneath you will follow suit. The fish rots from the head down, but the converse must also be true! Instead of cursing the darkness (and there's a lot of "darkness" out there when it comes to inept management!), light a candle and show others the way. Be the person you want *them* to be.

Of course, if you are okay with being a bully, a bloviator, or a bigwig, feel free, but know that those "beneath" you will be affected by your behavior—and your words.

When a Manager Avoids Confrontation

Gentle

- Trust me, if you spare the rod, you'll spoil the team. [*joking*]
- The mark of a gifted manager is knowing when to reward them and when to give them a swift kick in the pants. [*joking*]
- Think of confrontation as a gift that you can give someone who deserves another chance.
- Think of this as an opportunity to bring out the best in your team.
- I know this is hard, but courage is feeling the fear and doing it anyway.
- I know how difficult some people can be, but you are the one they are all looking to for direction.
- It isn't easy to learn how to be the tough guy, but I promise it does get easier.
- What about this makes you uncomfortable? Maybe I can help talk you through it.
- Think of it this way: I'm doing it with you right now!
- Once they see you're willing to be the heavy, you'll have a lot less difficulty managing.
- There's a time and a season for everything, including laying down the law.
- I know it's not easy for you, but you need to get more comfortable with this part of your job.
- They are all looking to you to lead them. Can you do that?
- Your lack of leadership is causing problems on your team.
- If you don't acquire a backbone, your employees will run all over you.

Directive

- I can't force you to discipline your team; you have to learn that on your own.
- As a manager you're expected to be able to handle this kind of stuff.
- If you're unwilling to be the disciplinarian, perhaps this isn't the right position for you.
- No employee will respect a manager whose sole aim is to be liked.
- If you can't keep order within your team, I will need to write you up.
- How can you expect your team to perform well when *you* can't do your job?
- If you are that helpless I may as well get a babysitter for you, too.

When a Manager Isn't Leading Effectively

Encouraging

- I know you have it in you; now, show me what you can do!
- You are a gifted leader; you just need to put your natural abilities into practice.
- If I can learn how to lead well, anyone can!
- I can see that you're trying, but there is more that needs to be done in this area.
- I know you mean well, but this is an area that needs some improvement.
- Nobody is a born leader. It takes a lot of practice and a willingness to fail.
- A lot of this will be trial and error, but you have to be willing to get your hands dirty.
- They are looking to you for direction, and you need to step up and give it to them.

Punitive

- This position requires real leadership. Are you equal to the task?
- You are going to need to step up and be more accountable as a leader.
- A rudderless ship is destined to founder. Is that what you want?
- There are leaders and there are followers, and it looks as though you will always be a follower.
- I'm not sure you're the right person for this job anymore.
- The fish rots from the head down, you know.
- You need to lead already or just step down.

When a Manager Micromanages

Subtle

- Are you comfortable with the way you are overseeing everything? Why or why not?
- You must be exhausted, having to watch everyone like a hawk all day long.
- A team that has room to innovate is the best kind of team to lead.
- There's nothing that pleases employees more than being trusted to do a good job.
- If you give your team a little breathing room, I think you'll be pleasantly surprised at the results.
- The more empowered your team, the more effective you will be as a manager.
- I know you are anxious, but you need to relax and let your people find their own level.
- Do you not trust your people? Why would you hire people you don't trust?

Directive

- Micromanaging is like a rocking chair: There's a lot of movement, but it never gets you anywhere.
- By micromanaging you are telling your people that you don't believe in them.
- How will you ever know what your team is capable of if you never give them a chance?
- Your management style is a bit–how shall I say it?–stifling.
- We are all professionals here; no one needs to be babysat.
- Your people have complained that they feel as though Big Brother is watching them.
- Micromanaging will never guarantee success. Empowering your employees will.
- I trust you to do a good job; now, accord that same respect to your team.
- I appreciate your commitment, but you need to lay off the micromanagement tactics.
- Smothering your team will not put you in their good graces.
- Your team knows what they're doing; they don't need you to hold their hands all the time.
- I've heard that life in your department is like life under a microscope. Is this true?
- Relax, Mr. Manager. If you've hired the right team, they'll get the job done.
- You are slowly killing your team's morale, investment, and motivation.
- I'm not sure your management style is a good fit here anymore.
- Either the micromanaging stops or I'm going to have to replace you.

When a Manager Cannot Delegate

Subtle

- The best managers are those who recognize and use each employee's special skills.
- Being a great leader is like conducting an orchestra: The conductor doesn't play *all* the parts.
- My favorite managers have always been those who use everyone's unique strengths.
- You're obviously invested in your work, but others need to be involved, too.
- Maybe you need to let go a little and let your people do their jobs.
- Delegation is difficult for capable people like you, but you may just be surprised at the results.
- I know you think you can do it better, and you probably can, but that's not an effective way to manage.
- If you never delegate, your team will feel as though you don't trust them to finish anything.
- If you want to take on all the work yourself, why pay the salaries of all those people on your team?
- Being able to delegate is liberating and, ultimately, much more effective in the long run.
- Managers who don't involve their team in the work soon won't have a team to involve.
- A manager who can't delegate isn't a manager. She is an automaton.
- Some people on your team are starting to call you a control freak. What do you think of that?
- Nobody likes a manager who hogs all the interesting work.
- No one here is indispensible—not even you.
- No one is doing anything in your department but you, yet they're all getting paid. Why is that?

Directive

- If you can't delegate, you'll eventually burn out and completely demoralize your team in the process.
- I have no use for a manager who refuses or is unable to delegate.
- Either you fix this or you're out.

When a Manager Is Bullying Subordinates

Gentle

- Do your employees seem happy to you? Can you think of a reason why that might be?
- Don't you see how miserable your people are?
- Do you think you get the best from a team that is miserable and demoralized?
- You inspire fear but not respect. Is that what you want?
- Don't you think it's unfair to pick on those who are less powerful than you?
- There is a huge difference between being authoritative and being authoritarian.
- There is an old saying: "Walk softly but carry a big stick."
- I think you need a little more carrot and a little less stick.
- I know you think you're helping, but look at how unhappy your people are.
- You can catch more flies with honey than you can with vinegar.
- Here's a hint: It's in *your* best interest to treat your people with respect.
- Positive reinforcement is much more effective than put-downs and abuse.

- Your approach may work in the short term, but you have to think long term, here.
- There is a big difference between being directive and just being a bully.
- If you treat your people this way, how can you expect them to treat each other well?
- I can't understand why you would ever think that bullying your subordinates is okay.
- Your people may not be able to stand up to you, but I will be more than happy to do so on their behalf.
- I think you need to think long and hard about your need to always put people down.
- This company is a bully-free zone—or maybe you didn't get that memo?
- Watch your step. You may end up on the receiving end of that kind of treatment someday.
- Do you have any idea how brutal you are with others? Maybe we need to record you.
- You need to lighten up before someone takes out a bounty on your head.
- Take a hint, Caesar: There's a little bit of Brutus in every subordinate.
- Congratulations on completely ruining any chance you and your team ever had for success here. [*sarcasm*]
- I will not tolerate your demoralizing your team in this manner. Either cut it out or get out.

Harsh

When a Manager Is Too Laissez-Faire

Gentle

- If I were you, I would need a bit more structure in my team's daily routine.
- I know you trust your people, but you need to also show them that you care about results.
- A certain amount of centralized leadership always seems to help keep things on track.
- I know you like things relaxed around the office, but where is the productivity?
- Your lack of energy and investment is contagious. Do you realize that?
- I know you're a laid-back kind of person, but how will any work ever get done?
- Your workers definitely like you, but I wonder if you have their respect.
- What would you think of being a bit tighter with your expectations, going forward?
- Don't be afraid to be the bad guy sometimes; they will respect you for it later.
- When everyone is in charge, no one is in charge.
- As a manager you have a great deal of power here, if you'd only use it.
- Holding people accountable is a necessary part of management; I suggest you try it.
- I'm not sure your management style is effective; perhaps we could talk about that.
- Your people are running all over you and making you look bad. Don't you care?
- "Laissez-faire" is the opposite of "do your share." Understand?
- Some managers have a wishbone where their backbone ought to be.

Harsh

- Your inability to take charge is killing your chances for success.
- There's nothing wrong with being laid back, but your team is completely taking advantage of you.
- Why should we keep paying you to basically do nothing here?
- You are fiddling while Rome burns.
- I don't see how I can entrust an entire department to someone who obviously cares so little.

When a Manager Is Too Friendly With the Team

Gentle

- It's good that you care about your team, but it's important to keep those boundaries intact.
- I think we can strike a better balance between friendliness and respect. What do you think?
- If you are all buddy-buddy with your team, how will you be able to discipline them?
- I would be more comfortable if you were more objective with your team.
- You need to understand that a real leader is an authority figure, not a friend.
- A overly friendly/intimate leadership style rarely produces stellar results.
- If you get too close with your crew, you will lose your ability to think objectively.
- A "fraternity" management style is not the best approach, here
- You're getting too close to your team for your—and their—own good.
- We don't recommend fraternizing with one's direct reports; it just creates too many problems.

Harsh

- You can't lead *and* hang out with your team at the same time. It just doesn't work.
- A true leader helps his team achieve greatness; what you're doing is called fraternization.
- Your excessive closeness to your team is being perceived as a sign of weakness.
- Being that intimate with one's inferiors is demeaning to them and to you.
- You really need to put some professional distance between you and your team.
- If you were any closer to your team you'd be borrowing their clothes.
- You're much too close to your subordinates and it's getting in the way of work.
- Either you start acting like a manager or you're out.

When a Manager Is Playing Favorites

Subtle

- Everyone here needs to feel that they're equally engaged with leadership.
- I'd like to see your enthusiasm and investment extend to *all* your team members.
- It's natural to gravitate toward certain people, but as a manager you need to remain fair and unbiased.
- Can you think of a reason why some employees may be feeling unappreciated or neglected?
- When employees feel ignored or underappreciated, it has a negative effect on morale.

- You have a lot of talent on your team that you aren't putting to good use.
- Your *whole* team needs to know that you have their backs, not just your favorites.
- It's important that you invest in each member of your team, not just a select few.
- I think if you stepped back from the situation you'd realize you're being unfair to the rest of the team.
- If you focus on an "inner circle" while excluding the rest, the whole team will suffer.
- Playing favorites isn't fair to anyone, especially you!
- Doling out preferential treatment just makes you look weak and ineffective.
- Leadership is not about establishing cliques, playing favorites, or being in the "in" crowd.
- You may not realize this, but your management style is alienating the majority of your team.
- You're being unfair to the rest of your team members and it needs to stop.
- I don't like the dynamic you've set up in your department; either something changes or you're out.

Directive

When a Manager Is Lazy

Polite

- It seems like you're in a bit of a rut; is there anything I can do to help?
- I sense a lack of motivation on your part; is it something I've done?
- I'm getting the sense that you're just not invested in your work. What's going on?
- You seem to take the way of least resistance pretty often; can you tell me why that might be?
- Look, I wish I could coast through my days, too, but there's a lot more at stake here than our comfort.
- Everyone hits the wall occasionally, but you've got to shake it off and get back to work.
- I know it's difficult, but you've got to keep your nose to the grindstone.
- I understand that you're not feeling the love, but you've got a team to manage.
- I sense a lack of urgency and commitment coming from you.
- If you don't get back into the groove, I sense a rocky road ahead for you.
- Tell me why I should continue to invest in a manager who doesn't care.
- Your abysmal work ethic is infecting this entire company; I can't have that.
- Lose the lazy attitude, okay?
- I'm not paying you to show up and do nothing; get it together or you're through.
- Please, share with me your secret to eternal idleness. [sarcasm]
- I so rarely get to meet a man of leisure. However do you do it? [sarcasm]

Rude

- Do you ever think you'll find it in yourself to get some work done? [*sarcasm*]
- You need to man up and get back to work, or I'm done with you.
- You've become a dead weight here, so I have no choice but to fire you.

Bonus Section
Managing Up

Creativity takes courage.
–Henri Matisse

Management is rarely a one-way street. In fact, much of your time as a manager will be spent "managing" your superiors. You'll need to learn how to leverage responses and behavior–whether subtly or overtly–from your higher-ups. Caution: this is not for the meek. This kind of managing takes practice, creativity, and, sometimes, courage. It's not for the novice. All of us can feel powerless at times when it comes to interacting with those who sign our paychecks. If you've ever felt this way, this section is definitely for you!

How to Say No to a Superior

Gentle

- I can see it's important to you; can I try tackling it later, once I'm free?
- I wish you had asked me earlier, before these other tasks were dumped on my desk!
- Right now I'm working on that other project you gave priority to. Should I stop doing that?
- Well, right now I'm doing X; which of these tasks is more important to you?
- I want to say yes so badly, but right now I'm completely committed to this other project.
- Not right now, but I'd be more than happy to do it at a later date.
- I wish I could say yes, but unfortunately I can't.
- That doesn't sound like something I'll be able to do, unfortunately.
- I can't do that, but I would be willing to do X instead.
- I won't be able to do that for you, sorry.
- Sorry, no can do.
- You can't be serious.
- No.
- No way, José!
- Fire me if you want to, but I'm not doing that.

Blunt

How to Ask for a Raise

- Have you noticed how well my department is doing lately?
- I really want to know if you are happy with my performance here.
- How do you feel I've been doing, given all of our recent success?
- Please let me tell all the great things I've been accomplishing lately!
- I'd like to revisit my pay scale at some point this week, if that's okay with you.
- Ultimately it's your decision, and I don't want to pressure you, but a raise would mean a lot to me.
- Do you think that I might deserve a raise, given all my accomplishments this past year?
- I believe have demonstrated all the qualities of a manager who deserves a raise. What do you think?
- I know you appreciate me, but I'd like to see that backed up with something more concrete.
- I'd like more responsibility as well as an increase in pay to go with it.
- Why do I deserve a raise? Here's a list of 10 reasons why.
- My pay should be commensurate with my performance; wouldn't you agree?
- My record here is stellar. Don't you think I deserve a little something for all I've done?
- Why am I not making as much as others who aren't performing as well as I am?
- It's okay if you won't give me a raise. There are other options out there if it comes to it.

Direct

- Look, I'm either worth it or I'm not. Which is it?
- I know how valuable I am, even if this company doesn't.
- It's not about the money; it's about what's fair.

How to Run Interference for Your Team

Noncommittal

- Look, I know they're fumbling, but give them a chance.
- Obviously they have a long way to go, but I have hope.
- Please be patient while I work out the glitches they've been having.
- What about my team upsets you so much? Maybe I can help mediate the situation.
- I wish they were doing better, too. I blame myself.
- Yes, but the jury is still out on the results. Give them more time.
- They are doing the best they can with the resources they've been given.
- I know it looks bleak right now, but hang in there a bit longer; I know they can do it.
- You don't know them like I do; I believe their best is yet to come.
- I can assure you my team will outperform all the others, come crunch time.
- I consider myself their advocate when it comes to upper management; so, what's your gripe?
- Nobody gets to my team unless they go through me first.
- I would bet my life on this team. You just don't have enough faith yet.

Vociferous

- I will never let anyone degrade my team, especially not to their faces–or mine.
- Since they are my responsibility, you'll need to talk to *me* about what's bothering you.
- If you want to deal with my team you'll have to deal with *me*.
- My team and I are as thick as thieves; no higher-up is going to get in the middle of that.
- I will defend my team with everything in my power until I am no longer with this company.

How to Discuss Your Team's Mistake

Conscientious

- All I can say is *mea culpa*.
- As their manager I take full responsibility for the mistake; it will never happen again.
- They were just following my orders, so the blame rests squarely on me.
- The fish rots from the head down, so I am the culprit here.
- Whatever happened was my fault, so please talk to me about it.
- I take responsibility for my group's error. More than that I cannot do.
- They were just the messengers; don't blame them!
- They are partly to blame, but only in that they didn't execute my orders perfectly.
- At the end of the day we were *all* responsible for what went wrong.

Blaming

- I am so sorry for the way my team performed. I just don't know what happened.
- There is nothing at all I can do except say I'm sorry.
- I try my damnedest to bring out the best in them and *this* is what happens!
- My team made a horrendous error. I hope we can all accept that and move on.
- When I look back on what my people did, it won't be the highlight of my career.
- I thought they had it all together, but they totally blew it.
- I did the best I could; I can't help it if they are useless.
- Hey, it's not my fault they screwed up.

How to Deal With a Bully Boss

Conciliatory

- Because I admire you so much, I wish things between us were more civil.
- I respect you enormously, but I wish we could speak to one another more civilly.
- Speaking for myself, I'd prefer a more collaborative spirit in our interactions.
- You will catch more flies with honey than you will with vinegar. [*joking*]
- You have so many strengths, but sometimes I wish you'd tone down your approach.
- Your communication style is a bit—how shall I say this?—harsh at times.
- If you don't respect me, there is no way I'll be able to accord that same respect to you.

Confrontational

- Do you really feel that berating people is the way to get more out of them?
- You need to get a grip on your temper. It's not doing you any good at all.
- There is no reason at all to treat people the way you do. It's deplorable.
- I had no idea you were so difficult; if I had, I would have never chosen to work with you.
- It's because of you I can't sleep or have a normal life.
- Did someone above you mistreat you this way when *you* were climbing the corporate ladder?
- If you can't change the way you speak to me, I'll have to move on.

How to Request a Project

Subtle

- It's probably not possible for me to request that assignment, is it?
- Hmm, that new project looks pretty cool; did you have anyone specific in mind?
- If I got a chance to work on this, I'd be so excited!
- I'd love to sit down with you at some point and hash out our plans for my next project.
- I believe that new project would suit my abilities pretty well. What do you think?
- I think I'd be a good fit for that new assignment. Would you be comfortable with my requesting it?

Declarative

- I realize that my assignments are largely out of my control, but can we discuss some possibilities?
- With your concurrence, of course, I'd love to show you what I can do with this project.
- That new assignment has me salivating. Any chance you would be willing to put in my name for it?
- Is there any way I could put in my name for this project? I'm really interested!
- I know you value initiative, which is why I'm officially putting my name in for that new project.
- I am dying for a shot at that new project; don't make me beg!

How to Introduce a New Idea

Subtle

- I'm not really an idea person, but would you care to hear this crazy notion I had anyway?
- Obviously your ideas are much closer to the mark, but what would we think of X?
- If you are interested in hearing what I think, please let me know.
- I'd like to give you my take on this, but I don't want to step on anyone's toes.
- This may be crazy, but what would you think of X?
- I'm wondering if anyone ever considered doing X instead?
- What would you think of brainstorming some new ideas? I have one that may just be feasible.

Overt

- I have a new idea that I'd like to discuss with you. Are you available this week?
- Since I know you value innovation, I'd like to tell you about an idea I have.
- Okay, here's an idea—but feel free to shoot it down, okay?
- I wish we could at least consider X as a possibility. What do you think?
- I had a flash of insight about this the other day. Curious?
- I have what I think is a pretty good idea; are you interested in hearing more?
- I can guarantee you'll want to go with this idea; it's that good!

When You Need a Lighter Workload

Subtle

- We need to share tasks more effectively here. Isn't that what teamwork is all about?
- Is there a chance that someone else could take a task or two off my plate?
- Is there any way you can help me delegate some of these tasks to other people?
- I think I would be more effective if I delegated some of this work to my team members.
- I really thought I could handle all this work, but I think I bit off more than I could chew.
- I'm not saying I can't do it all, only that I won't be able to get it all done at once.
- I've been feeling a bit overwhelmed lately and I'd like to brainstorm some solutions with you.

Blunt

- My intent is to finish everything I started, but I can't do that if I'm given more work.
- Everyone has their limit, and I think I may have already reached mine.
- I am only one person, you know.
- I believe I have reached a level of commitment beyond which I simply cannot go.
- My plate is overfull to the point of distraction. I'm going to need your help with this.
- Frankly, I'm feeling overwhelmed, and I'm wondering what can be done about it.
- I'm not too proud to admit that I have taken on more than I can handle.
- I feel like I'm drowning here, and I'm going down fast unless someone helps me out!
- If I don't get some help with all this, I am going to burn out, and fast!
- I know I can count on you to back me up, here. I just can't do any more!

How to Flatter a Superior

Subtle

- I'm trying not to be too intimidated, here. [*joking*]
- Spending some time among the minions/rabble/ madding crowd, are we? [*joking*]
- Ah, it's good to be the king. [*joking*]
- I'd really love to bend your ear at some point.
- I want to learn everything I can from you.
- I have a great deal to learn from you; I can see that.

- Speaking frankly, your level of experience is bit daunting to me.
- If I could only choose one person to mentor with, it would be you.
- Have you ever written a book? You really should.
- There are very few people who are actually indispensable; you are one of them.
- I wish I were as knowledgeable/experienced/talented as you.
- There are people of mere words and people of action; clearly you are the latter.
- I've seen you around, but you are much more distinguished/intelligent/intimidating in person.
- You make it look so easy. How do you do it?
- Yes, I am flattering you, but in this case it's warranted!

Overt/Obvious

How to Disagree With a Superior

- I'm wondering if we should look at this some other way.
- I don't want to step on any toes, but I'm wondering if we should revisit this.
- Far be it for me to disagree with you, but what if considered this instead?
- Can I play devil's advocate here for just a moment?
- If only for the sake of argument, let's consider this alternative for a moment.
- While you definitely have a point, I'm not entirely sure that's right.

Conciliatory

Blunt

- Ordinarily I would agree with you, but not this time.
- I'm sorry, but I'm going to have to disagree with you on this one.
- I don't agree, and here's why.
- I think you'll have to concede that I'm right this time.
- Your position just isn't defensible.
- Just because you are saying it doesn't mean it's true.
- You are *way* off!

How to Ask for a Vacation

Circuitous

- Where did you go on your vacation again?
- I can't even remember the last time I took a real vacation.
- Joe in accounting just said he needs a vacation; don't we all! [*joking*]
- I bet you're looking forward to your vacation. Speaking of which...
- Now that I've finished my projects, I'm wondering if this would be an opportune time for a break.
- Do you think I should take a vacation at some point? I'm feeling a little burned out.
- I'll be much more productive once I get a chance to recharge my batteries.
- I want to run some dates by you so that I can schedule some much-needed down time.

Direct

- When would be a good time for me to take a vacation?
- I don't think it's unreasonable for me to take some time off, do you?
- I'd like to take some time off, if that's okay with you. Let me know what dates would work best.
- I'm taking these dates off; let me know if this poses a problem for you.
- It would really be a shame if I couldn't take some time off, considering how much time you've taken.

When You Feel Overworked

Circuitous

- I guess this is what Red Bull was invented for, huh? [*joking*]
- Sometimes I feel like I sleep here, you know?
- I know work can get intense, but right now I don't see an end in sight.
- I know I'm a mess; I'm just tapped out here, it seems.
- I simply can't add another thing to my plate; I'm that burned out.
- I'm trying to muster more stamina, but at this point I don't think I have it in me.
- You know I'd do anything for this company, but not at the risk to my own health.
- Remember the last time you felt overworked? Let me tell you, I'm about there myself.

- I think we'll all working way too hard, myself included.
- I am so overworked that I'm afraid I am no longer as productive as ought to be.
- I'm so worn out I find myself not even caring anymore, which really scares me.
- I think we need to revisit my workload; I feel like I'm buckling underneath the weight of it.
- I have just about reached the limit of what I can bear, here.
- I don't mind working hard, but this is ridiculous!
- Nobody should have work under these sorts of conditions. It's inhuman.

Blunt

Index

About the Author

Patrick Alain is an internationally known video game developer. His titles include the number-one bestsellers "Grand Theft Auto," "Red Dead Redemption," and the *Midnight Club* series. He was born in Paris, France, and has lived in a number of countries throughout his life. Fluent in five languages, Alain attributes much of his success to his ability to function as a vital participant in large, multilingual teams. This book is the product of more than 10 years of experience in management. It is Alain's goal to share his knowledge regarding one of the most invaluable skills in life: *taking command in every situation.*

Alain lives in San Diego, California, with his wife and daughter. He holds a master's degree from the University of Paris.

PatrickAlain.com   Twitter.com/LeaderPhrases